*A Guide to Gardening
to Attract Wild Birds*

THE
WILD BIRD
GARDEN

*A Guide to Gardening
to Attract Wild Birds*

THE
WILD BIRD
GARDEN

LESLIE JACKMAN

Illustrated by
JAYNE NETLEY

SOUVENIR PRESS

First published 1992 by Souvenir Press Ltd,
43 Great Russell Street, London WC1B 3PA
and simultaneously in Canada

ISBN 0 285 63085 7

Printed in Hong Kong and bound in China through Bookbuilders Ltd

CONTENTS

LIST OF ILLUSTRATIONS

1
THE GREEN WORLD
BEYOND THE GARDEN

A bird, much like any other animal, is entirely dependent upon habitat. Whilst it is obvious that woodpeckers need trees and kingfishers need water, trees and water are by no means their sole requirements but simply the outstanding essential features. A whole amalgam of other factors contributes to where and when you might expect to find any particular bird, for each bird is but a single link in a complex chain.

A bird reacts with everything around it, and it is sensitive to the world in which it lives in ways we are barely beginning to understand. Its involvement with its total environment is so close that everything within it is a living part of its entire life-style.

A bird is able to recognise and will react with any immediate signals it receives from its surroundings at any given time. From all these—perhaps mostly visual—signals, it recognises those which are reliable indicators that other basic needs will be satisfied. For example, a bird of the deciduous woodland, which tends to be associated with oak, will first respond to the outline and general contours of an oak tree and will then ensure that other important factors are present: a suitable nesting place, sufficient food to rear its young, a place to drink and the presence or absence of other animals, including, of course, birds of its own species; and always a tree or bush from which to proclaim in song. The absence of any one of these factors may well cause the bird to move on.

It is obvious from this that a bird investigates its chosen habitat in quite considerable detail. It knows its way about within it; knows where the food is, where water is available for drinking and washing and where predators may lurk. Such recognition involves senses other than sight. The scent of certain trees, unrecognisable to us, may give profound signals, as may the sound of a spring or stream and even the smell of water in half-hidden pools, for the senses of birds are sensitive beyond our imagination.

It would appear that habitat recognition is innate within the bird, yet there is nevertheless an element of learning involved, as, for instance, when a habitat is destroyed and an immediate need arises to find a place that, although *slightly* different, will still supply its basic needs.

In this connection it is interesting to note that the vast spread of monocultural cereal crops, whilst providing limitless grain as a food, did not offer trees as singing and nesting sites because the hedgerows had been removed, and in consequence grain-feeding finches did not increase but rather did they decline.

If all the foregoing applies to the wild green world and is essential in habitat selection, it is similarly important in our gardens. Birds respond to every feature in our garden just as they do in the wild—hence the importance of creating habitat

A cock chaffinch sings from a conspicuous perch in a tree, both to attract a female and to repel other cocks.

and thus supplying features which are of psychological importance to the bird but which to us may seem to have little ecological relevance.

HABITAT AND THE SEASONS

Familiar as we are with the coming of spring, we have only the barest perception of what it must mean to the birds. For them, the long, pitiless winter has been a wearying struggle for survival: seeking food, shelter from wind, protection from rain; fluffing feathers at night to ward off the energy-sapping frost. Then, suddenly, it is spring again. There is a scent of life rising into the trees, the first celandine and maybe an early tortoiseshell butterfly aroused from hibernation by the fragile warmth of the sun. Even for mere humans, it is a time of renewal, a great celebration of winter's departure.

For the birds, however, it is a period of physical release as their bodies respond to rhythms as old as time, and in the bird garden we become aware of a growing liveliness. Blue tits had already prospected potential nest sites way back when the fieldfares took the last of the holly berries; now blackbirds noisily contest territory, flinging themselves from bushes to see off intruders; the sparrow colony becomes vociferous and highly interactive.

And everywhere around us, whether in city or countryside, are intimate relationships between the plants and animals living within the structure of the environment—their habitat. Unless it reacts with us personally, we mostly ignore it; unless a motorway is planned to cut through our own patch, or there is some other equally disturbing alteration to our way of life, we tend to regard the pattern as unchangeable.

Spring comes with its sunshine and opening buds and we tune in to bird song; summer heat shimmers on beach and heathland and we relax in the scented dusk; autumn gilds the woodland and we scent the dying year; winter mist and frost paint the gossamer spider's webs and we pause to wonder. To each of us the passing seasons are seen according to our mood. But to wildlife the changing scene is intensely dramatic and for birds a matter of survival; the nature and composition of their habitat are crucial. Tidy up a woodland, and woodpecker nest sites and feeding places are destroyed; plough up old grassland, and lark song diminishes; grub out hedgerows, and the dunnock and greenfinch become homeless.

Indeed, a woodland, a hedgerow or a meadow are never unchanged for a single day. Life and death are happening all around; growth and decay inevitably change the scene; colours, scents and sounds intensify, merge and fade, for that is a vital part of our world and the interaction between the living and non-living.

No matter whether you live in the greenest of wild country or the artificial fastness of a great city, you will share the environment with birds, for birds are great survivors and if driven from a familiar habitat they will first seek another similar one that offers all their requirements, or, and this is more often the case, will move to somewhere less favourable and try to adapt to the conditions prevailing there.

Some years ago, I witnessed a kingfisher trying to cope with the destruction of its habitat. For many years a pair had enjoyed a small stream that was a tributary to the nearby main river. Each year they nested in the bank where meadowsweet and wild iris flowered in season, and the bed of the stream had a plentiful growth of water dock, water crowfoot, hornwort and milfoil. Trout fry and sticklebacks swam there, and a host of insect larvae. Plentiful food and lack of disturbance provided the ideal habitat.

But one autumn the motorway constructors moved in with huge cement pipes and channelled away part of the stream. The kingfishers disappeared. The following spring, quite by chance, I passed the site where bulldozers, cement-mixers and construction huts had taken over the water meadows, and there, perched on a baulk of timber where the free-running stream plunged into the pipes, was the kingfisher. It must have been weighing up the potential of the devastated site, but that summer the nest site was abandoned. Adaptation in this case was obviously quite impossible and it provided one more demonstration of the importance of habitat.

More optimistically, many species are benefiting from our consciousness of their needs and our place in the world we share with them. And nowhere is this more apparent than in the great upsurge of garden interest that has blossomed during the past twenty years. For the birds, this has created a great opportunity for exploration and a very considerable extension of habitat.

HABITAT PREFERENCES

There is little doubt that the breeding success of many of our garden birds depends upon our understanding of their wild and natural life-styles, and often the simplest of alterations to our existing garden will have the most gratifying results. Whilst it may be beyond the capacity of a small garden to replicate all the facets of a natural oak wood community, enough of the essential ingredients can be supplied to attract some of the birds that live there.

Generally speaking, deciduous and mixed woodland are a favoured habitat of great tit, song thrush, redstart, robin, chaffinch, wood pigeon, blue tit and wren. Some of these species are also found in coniferous and mixed woodland along with coal tits. Farmland hedges with grassland, scrub, borders of woods and cultivated land are home to greenfinch, magpie, house sparrow, collared dove and crow; the dunnock hides away in spinneys, hedgerows and bushy places, whilst blackbirds and starlings occur almost anywhere.

A helpful understanding of how we can adapt our garden to the needs of a particular species can be gained by considering the delightful, acrobatic blue tit, familiar to everyone and a joy to watch. Whilst most gardens are visited by this bright little bird, the vast majority of the species live and remain within their natural habitat, deciduous woodland, where often more than one breeding pair per acre may be found. Many of these make winter visits into the suburbs and towns where human-provided food may be more abundant than that offered by the trees. With the onset of spring, some stay on to nest in the boxes we provide, but most return to the woods to seek out crevices and holes in trees, which are their natural nest sites. Blue tits have a close attachment to oak trees and these are certainly their favourite foraging areas.

If you go into an oak wood in early summer and make yourself comfortable by sitting at the base of a tree, it will not be long before you see these little birds at work. Their acrobatic tendencies can be seen being put to good use as they cling to twigs, upside-down, to inspect the underside of leaves where the caterpillars are hiding. And caterpillars are consumed in enormous quantities: if we assume that as many as one hundred thousand caterpillars are in a single large oak, a pair of blue tits may consume and take to their nestlings upwards of ten thousand in a single season. That represents a considerable effort and degree of skill on the tiny bird's part.

Despite the camouflage of those larvae, the tits find them and even recognise and ignore those with particularly noxious hairs or body fluids—no poor achievement considering that throughout an average season there is a continuous succession of moth larvae, numbering dozens of species. Loopers, disguised as tiny twigs, green larvae stretched along leaf ribs, others the colour and texture of the lichens on the bark—a host of shapes, sizes and, to tits, delectability, is searched out, seized and consumed. As you watch you will become more and more aware of the blue tits' close affinity with the trees. Seldom do they explore the lower bushes, and almost never flit around near the ground. In fact, if you see one alight on the woodland floor you will have had an almost unique experience.

But tits, like other birds, seek out a fairly comprehensive diet which is extremely flexible: their food includes the fruits of moss and elderberries, and quite frequently they break open some of the oak galls which, in season, contain juicy larvae and pupae of the gall wasps. Then, as autumn advances, the survivors of the enormous population of caterpillars have pupated and/or emerged and so the little birds come in to our gardens for nuts and fat and remain for the winter; for although there is still food to be found in the woodland it is no longer abundant and is insufficient to support the large tit population that has thrived there during the summer months.

How, then, does this experience of blue tits in the wild habitat help us when we return home? Certainly it should have started us thinking. One very obvious factor is the birds' liking for the trees. To what extent can we replicate this in our garden? Can we find room for a tree, two trees or more? How close to the natural species can we select our tree or trees? Depending on how impatient we are, how long are we prepared to wait for the tree to grow? Fortunately for the birds, most gardeners are patient people.

Next time you visit the wood it may be nesting time. Look carefully and try to determine at what height they choose their nest holes. Yes, I know the information is all in the books and that specific instructions are outlined for dimensions, placing, entrance hole sizes and so on, but it is surely much more enjoyable to discover such facts by observation in the wild.

We live in a world of clocks, schedules, noise and crowding, and we become so used to it that we tend to forget the green world just beyond our house. Visiting a quiet wood and spending an hour there listening to bird song and watching the birds is a wonderful vitaliser. You will return home not only refreshed in body but awakened and aware of the green world and its relationship with yourself.

Another day, why not spend a while leaning on a gate, watching a hedge? If possible choose a site where two sides of a field meet so that you get the double advantage of two hedges. Try to find a hedge that has not been 'massacred' by modern slash cutters, for although this method often thickens up the subsequent growth and so provides nest sites for some species, in general terms you will find more birds in 'wild' hedges.

If you keep very still you will probably get a brief glimpse of a dunnock, but the best indicator of its presence is the faint peep-peep call from a dense, dark clump of undergrowth. Blackbird and chaffinch may be seen as they fly into the field to feed; perhaps a linnet or a pair of yellowhammers and a robin or white-throat flying along the hedge. You will possibly see a few butterflies that are

Thickets, tall hedges and gardens with trees are the sort of habitat greenfinches favour. From late autumn into early winter they enjoy rosehips and even a few blackberries (female on right).

particularly attracted to such sites: in May or July and August the wall butterfly basking in the sun on a blackberry leaf, whereas on the shadowed side of the hedge, the flitting form of a speckled wood; as a first sign of spring, flying fast towards you the beautiful orange tip. Each according to season and with them the birds that share the habitat.

As you rest by the gate and listen to the bird song, take a closer look at the plants, from the occasional tall oak or sycamore to the denser hazel bushes down to the ferns, on the shaded side, to the flowers thrusting out of the hedge and the dandelions flashing their suns in the hedge bottom. Look at how the honeysuckle twines around the hazel; how the ivy climbs the oak trunk; how old man's beard rises on pliant 'vines' high into a sycamore where it drapes over in a waterfall of leaves; see the blackberry thicket where the grasses thrust their pendent stems, and the wild rose over-arching hardheads, goose grass, delicate stitchwort and bright campions.

This is the sort of habitat you too can create. Simply copy nature within the space you have available, selecting your plants and grouping them as happens in the wild. If you feel it is all too difficult, look at a field corner or piece of waste-ground and notice how the plants have colonised it. What nature does naturally, you may copy successfully, always providing you observe closely how it all happens.

Some time ago, as the result of elm disease, we lost our garden hedge, so in order to replace those trees we planted a variety together with a lime. The latter was chosen for its rich source of honey and pollen, but it soon became obvious that it was a meeting place of blue tits which spent much time flitting among the branches before visiting the bird table. It seemed to be a natural site for a nest box. One duly installed was occupied and a family reared. There was an unexpected bonus: lime hawk moths laid their eggs and dozens of their lovely caterpillars fed, grew and pupated—incidentally replacing the poplar hawk moths that for many years had bred in a tall lombardy poplar that overgrew its situation and had to be felled. Lime hawk moths and tits in exchange for the loss of poplar hawk moths and elms—a simple example of the importance of losing one and gaining another habitat. For even a single tree may prove a valuable habitat for smaller forms of life. Admittedly, this experience happened by chance, but a whole lot more will happen in *your* garden as long as you keep your eyes open and observe the birds' way of life in their natural, wild habitat.

Your bird visitors are, in a sense, country cousins up for the day, and a thorough understanding of their natural, green lives is essential if we are ever to succeed in attracting more and more species to our gardens. And there is absolutely no doubt that they do go visiting, especially when a food source dries up and the need for fresh pastures becomes urgent. Two examples are the way goldfinches seek out thistles in late summer, and jays flock to oaks when the acorns mature. And here at home, too, the bird garden provides a much needed source during the winter.

So it is that you will receive a constant stream of visitors to the garden, and the richer the variety of the required food and shelter you can provide, the longer will they stay. In his book *The Pattern of Animal Communities* Charles Elton says, 'The frequent dependence of birds upon structural features of the habitat that do not seem to have much immediate ecological relevance . . . are a psychological necessity for birds.' So, by getting to know the wild scene, you will understand, little by little, how to fulfil the birds' needs.

Successful bird gardening will be based upon the knowledge that your garden is a man-made habitat and that, whilst many birds have adapted to garden living, each will show individual preferences for certain gardens as opposed to others. This tendency is almost entirely due to their natural life-style in their wild environment, and their recognition of familiar features which draw them irresistibly to that place. Even a single tree may act as a signal, proclaiming food, and it is certain that we need to understand much more about any bird's reaction to natural features of many kinds. Whilst within these pages I have limited the number of bird species we loosely refer to as 'garden birds', the definition of 'garden' is totally *unlimited*. Your garden may range from a single peanut holder at the window of a city flat, through crumbs in a window box, small patios and suburban gardens to a green acre amidst open countryside.

But whatever the size of your patch and whatever it has to offer, all the birds that visit you are truly wild, their lives inextricably linked with their green and natural habitat.

Much of the pleasure in bird gardening lies in our simple ability to create a habitat which will attract both resident and migrant birds. There are of course limiting factors such as the nature of the immediate neighbourhood, its closeness to or distance from countryside and the degree of disturbance. However, only this week I watched some pigeons carrying on their life quite normally by preening on the window ledge of a church tower from which a full peal of bells was ringing out. So much for recognised disturbance! Birds learn quickly and even in the most unpromising area they will return again and again if the right conditions prevail.

IMPORTANCE OF HABITAT DIVERSITY

The size of the area is not nearly as important as its diversity of plants and other features, for the basic requirements of the birds are simple. One way to create variety is by seed-sowing, and fortunately many seed merchants now supply seeds that were once plentiful in the flowering countryside meadows. There, they attracted countless butterflies and provided a rich food source for birds, and their colourful flowers among the varied, delicate and beautiful grasses were typical of the countryside before monoculture moved in. Today they are making a comeback and our pleasure is enriched by their presence. In his book *The Ages of Gaia* James Lovelock referred to the England of his childhood: 'That landscape of England was no natural ecosystem; it was a *nation-sized garden* wonderfully and carefully tended.' A wonderfully rich bird habitat indeed.

The more diverse and varied the habitat, the greater the number of living species to be found there. Whilst in the creation of a bird garden the interests of the birds are of prime importance, the encouragement of insects, small mammals, snails, worms and many other creatures will contribute to your success. The web of life is an intricate mesh, involving many quite insignificant creatures and plants. It has been built up over countless eons of time and changes, man-made and natural, are happening all the while. Personally I am quite convinced that the planting of a nettle patch which then provides food for the larvae of tortoiseshell and red admiral butterflies interacts in a host of different ways with bird life. It is equally true that the use of certain sprays in the past, combined with the destruction of 'weeds', hedgerows and meadows, caused the decline of countless bird populations. It is beyond dispute that you and I are the most potent force for good or ill in the bird world, but thankfully bird gardens are proving a great force for good.

Gain and loss in the garden

I have already referred to the elm hedge in our own garden, which succumbed to Dutch elm disease. It was a very old, thick hedge which included one tall elm and a number of saplings, and its loss had a very considerable effect on the bird population in our garden. It was removed one autumn, and the following winter not a single greenfinch visited the bird table which was situated fairly close to the hedge site. Chaffinches, once so numerous at the table, declined in numbers until only one or two visited us each day. A pair of carrion crows which came to the tall elm in early spring to break off thin twigs for their nest in trees near the edge of the park, never visited the garden again. In previous years they had frequently flown in to feed. Another loss was the beautiful Jersey tiger moth whose larvae fed not only on the elm leaves, but also on the indigenous herbaceous plants that flourished in the hedge. The larvae hid beneath the fallen elm leaves during the day and spent the winter in the leaf litter shelter at the base of the hedge. We had had a colony of these in the garden for many years and become familiar with their colourful flights around midday. It was an isolated colony in a district where no others existed, and their loss represented a very real decline in the local population. In winter, passing bands of long-tailed tits always stayed awhile to explore the massed branches of our elm and their contact calls happily announced their presence. Many years passed before a band of those dainty tits reappeared. Now I realise that such happenings may have been triggered by other factors, but instinctively I know it was the demise of the elm hedge that caused the losses. In countless small ways it had contributed a micro-habitat that provided, through the varying seasons, simply those features that formed part of the life-style of the creatures that lived in it or visited it, no matter for how short a period.

CREATION OF HABITAT IN THE GARDEN

When thinking about the creation of living space for birds in your garden, the more obvious factors that you might consider—apart from the type of habitat you intend to achieve—are:

1 Position of garden in relation to surroundings.
2 Presence or absence of disturbance.
3 Type of terrain—hillside, damp areas, rocky places, new or old established site. Main features.

Carrion crows building nests near gardens often visit to collect twigs from trees such as silver birch. By supplying their needs we can all encourage more birds to visit us.

Perhaps equally important are your more personal wishes in relation to the garden—for instance, is it to be completely devoted to attracting birds or are you aiming for a compromise between a cultivated horticultural dream and a wild place? Do you perhaps want to provide only a feeding station?

Whatever your particular needs and preferences, the ideas in this book can be adapted or modified to suit them. Many of them are well proven and some are personal, but each in its own way will help create the bird attraction you want.

Position of garden in relation to surroundings
First of all, how about the land surrounding your garden? If, for instance it is very enclosed and built up you may well be able to provide an 'island sanctuary' for species passing through, which may then decide to stay a while, or even nest there. There is no doubt that birds can be extremely adaptable even in adverse

circumstances. A large housing estate built in once open country creates an entirely new kind of habitat and the spread of black redstarts in central London during the past sixty years demonstrates how a bird species can thrive in urban environments, whenever suitable terrain and habitat are created.

As a conservationist you will be aware of the importance of biological corridors linking habitats often of widely differing composition. Tree-lined roads, hedges, lanes and open fields between the wild world and your garden provide invaluable 'thoroughfares' for the birds. Alas, it is difficult to persuade some local authorities to conserve such open areas. There is so often an authoritarian attitude that likes tidiness as opposed to the random beauty of nature. Today it is pleasing to see more and more local councils not only rendering lip service to the green world but actually *doing* something about it. And that can only be good.

So, by approaching your local authority you may well encourage them to take conservation even more seriously and thus extend the connections between the wild, green world and your own garden. No matter how unpromising your situation, there are all sorts of interesting possibilities for someone prepared to 'have a go'.

Presence or absence of disturbance

Birds are extremely sensitive to noise, sudden movement or sudden change in habitat, but most of all they are wary of predators. In most gardens there will be a cat visitor or resident and without doubt the cat is the prime predator on garden birds. They represent a big problem chiefly because there is so little you can do to keep them out of your area. Cats wander from neighbouring 'territory' and have an unerring instinct to find easy bird prey, and they are so very, very patient as they hide under cover ready to attack. I have yet to find the answer. Of course there are the obvious measures we can all take in placing bird tables and nest boxes in cat-proof situations, but alas, this will not prevent the sad day when one dawn a cat climbs along the wall to a clump of bushes we so carefully planted and in which a bird has responded by nesting. The best we can do is to discourage cats whenever we see them in our bird garden for there is no way we can ever change their habits. They are too free-roaming, too independent of us and our ways.

Dogs, however, can be controlled more easily and even trained to leave birds well alone. If you own a dog and still want to have the birds, then a little judiciously placed fencing or trellis will provide a safe corner and still leave space for the dog. In the nesting season you will need to restrict its movements when the fledglings are about. Often young birds, for one of many reasons, explode out of the nest and land on the lawn or in the flowerbeds—and that sort of temptation often breaks the will-power of the best trained dog. Perhaps at that season you will be able to let the dog into the garden only when you are close by and watching. My apologies to dog and cat lovers. As I write, our springer is twitching at my feet because some trusting sparrows are hopping around the edge of the patio. She is trying hard to stay put, but it is a testing time, for she too regards this part of the garden as *her* territory, and sparrows are *so* provocative.

Type of terrain

Flat, rugged, sloping, marshy or sandy land all have potential, but the situation of your own house will be the governing factor. Nevertheless you can supply banks, hedges or rough ground providing you have room. Terrain in the garden and in its surrounding environment is important because it will prove attractive or unattractive to the species that are already present in the neighbourhood.

A few years ago our lawn was regularly visited by a green woodpecker which came for the ants that abounded there. It came from a woodland area separated from our garden by a crescent of meadows about half a mile wide. But the housing estate spread over the fields and within the next five years the bird's visits became fewer. Whilst the ants remain and woodpeckers still survive in the wood, they have never come back to our garden. On the other hand, our sparrows, being very local, were quite unaffected and indeed, since they thrive on all manner of unsuspected trifles, the presence of humans seems to have increased their numbers.

It is surprising how easy it is to make attractive areas by the judicious moving of soil, importing of stonework, hedge planting or by having a wild and natural place as well. Extremes, such as bare lawns surrounded by fences or bare brick walls, are as unlikely to attract birds as are square yards of cement. However, even in a tiny garden there will always be room for a bird table and drinking place which will bring life into an unpromising area, and small ponds enhance a formal paved patio by introducing reflections and attracting birds to bathe. The purchase of expensive materials, ornaments and the like never made as good a bird garden as thoughtful planning and imagination, for it is living plants and natural features that birds recognise and will come to share.

Apart from occasionally catching a bird, the local cat's presence in the garden discourages all but the boldest from flying in to feed, drink or bathe.

2
TREES, SHRUBS, BUSHES AND CLIMBERS

There is surely not a single garden that, with the very minimum of effort, cannot become richer in its variety of birdlife. With just a little knowledge gathered during woodland and country walks every one of us can apply our experiences to the garden that is ours. And, as in the wild, habitat will prove to be an invaluable asset.

A knowledge of the wild habitats of our garden birds will always form a firm basis for creating our bird garden, especially in selecting those plants most likely to prove attractive to them. For most small gardens the plants of the woodland edge, hedgerow and rough waste-ground are the best to choose and today, fortunately, more and more nurseries are making them available. In nature a bird may use a certain bush in which to build its nest, another from which to proclaim territory, yet another for roosting and a further series of plants for food. So no single plant will provide all the necessities for one species of bird throughout the year. Thus, to a limited extent, it is certain plants for certain birds, bearing in mind that, with a few occasional exceptions, berries are favoured by the larger birds and the less vigorous annual and perennial herbaceous plants provide seeds for the smaller ones. But one of the greatest assets we can offer the birds is plenty of cover, so select a few suitable bushes and, if there is space, one or two trees. Evergreens provide winter cover from rain, frost, snow and wind, whilst the deciduous shrubs may well supply a succession of food and, in the spring, a place to nest.

TREES AND SHRUBS FOR BERRIES

The importance of supplying berry-bearing shrubs cannot be over-emphasised. Did you know, for instance, that berries are so important to some species that they are guarded as a 'personal' food source? Many a blackbird thrives on cotoneaster and crataegus berries growing perhaps on adjacent bushes, and these it will defend from others as long as there are some berries remaining to be eaten.

It would be fascinating to discover just how a bird decides which particular food source it intends to guard, and that is another aspect of bird gardening which we will deal with later. There are many berry-bearing shrubs and trees which are particularly sought after by the birds, and whilst few of us can provide an oak tree rich in acorns which will bring in a flock of jays each autumn, we can still offer a variety of shrubs, bushes and trees to attract birds from the wild.

There is an added bonus for the wild bird gardener in the beauty of many of these plants, whose leaf shapes, blossom and berries all add their charm to the ever-changing seasons. There are more permutations to the choosing of groupings of trees and shrubs to suit *your* garden than there are berries on an elder in August, but that is all part of bird gardening. The following species can only form a basis for the later careful planning and creation of any particular site.

Amelanchier laevis.   June Berry

A hardy, easily grown tree producing an almost total covering of white flowers followed by massed pale red berries. As the tree grows year by year, so the visiting birds will feel more secure as they feed well above the ground out of the way of cats. Relaxed feeding inevitably means more birds, whereas in those areas where predators abound, they are always wary. And it is amazing how 'the word gets around' among the birds.

Amelanchier can be planted any time between November and late February, and whilst they enjoy a sunny or only partially shaded position, they thrive on moisture. They also require lime-free soil. They are best left unpruned, when they will grow to three metres in height, and when the birds come for the berries, the brilliant orange-red foliage will flame against the autumn sky.

Betula pendula.   Silver Birch

A graceful, beautiful tree that will thrive in a good loamy soil and can be planted any time during late autumn to early spring. Seeds should be sown in spring in any good quality seed compost and kept in either a cold frame or protected from cold weather, especially night frosts. As they grow to about five centimetres in height they should be transplanted into a row in a well-prepared garden bed and left to their own devices, except of course for weeding, for at least two years. They can then be put into their permanent situation, staked and generally cared for. Remember the importance of watering, especially if your soil tends to be sandy or otherwise dry. And why grow a silver birch? Well, apart from its beauty it will give a good crop of seeds just before the onset of winter and this may attract a variety of birds—perhaps a redpoll, if your garden is well planted with trees or close to a woodland. Siskins may visit, perhaps goldfinches and almost certainly some of the tits.

Corylus avellana.   Hazel

Grown naturally, the hazel makes an excellent bush for inclusion in a wild hedge, and whilst the male pendent flowers or catkins are obvious in early spring, the small red female flowers are quite inconspicuous and almost concealed in the buds. If kept coppiced, that is cut back almost to ground level each year, you will have a supply of plant stakes and the bush will re-grow. Hazel is so common in many hedgerows that it almost certainly forms part of the birds' recognition factor and in consequence attracts them to the garden.

Cotoneaster 'Cornubia'

A large-leaved standard bush growing up very slowly to around two metres and well worth its elegant place in the bird garden. A vigorous semi-evergreen, it will cover a wall area of up to six metres by six metres, with dark green leaves and massed creamy flowers during June. If encouraged to grow up some firm trellis or wires, it provides excellent cover for small birds, many of which explore its shady recesses for spiders and insects. From August to February its branches will be laden with round red fruits, thus providing a rich diet for birds during the cold months when natural foods are often in short supply. Mistle thrush and redwing, the latter a winter visitor to many lowland gardens, besides many semi-resident garden birds, will feed on them. It is one of the most favoured berry foods and a great attraction in any bird garden.

Cotoneaster horizontalis

Sometimes referred to as the herringbone cotoneaster, owing to its pattern of grey-green branches covered in small dark green and glossy leaves which turn colourful in autumn. This member of the rose family is ideal for covering a small bank or the top of a rockery where it will spread out to cover an area the size of a dinner table up to a modest height of less than 60 centimetres. Its bright green leaves will give autumn colour until they fall, and then in the winter those same leaves will be turned over by birds to reveal those 'unconsidered trifles' of insect life that too many gardeners regard as pests. If you want to clear away the leaves, that's fine, but the pink flowers of last June will have produced a crop of red berries all along the branches. Before they are consumed, those berries will brighten a shady wall with glints of summer past, although you will have to provide fixings to encourage it to abandon its 'horizontalis' attitude and grow up to about two metres.

Crataegus monogyna.   Hawthorn, May, Quickthorn, Whitethorn

A tall bush, which each year is associated with bird legend. You must have heard people say, 'Look at all those berries, we are going to have a hard winter!' A Dartmoor farmer's wife I know believes that 'plenty of berries, the birds will be all right, they do say God provides'. Biologists might tell you that the number of berries is dependent upon the weather conditions prevailing at pollination time back in spring. Whatever you choose to believe, they are grand bird plants.

This very common hedgerow tree attains a height of ten metres but can be kept within reasonable bounds by careful pruning. Since it will not grow easily from cuttings you are faced with two choices: buy an established pot-grown bush from a garden centre or collect your own seed. Seed should be gathered when the berries are ripe during October and if sown in an untreated condition take up to 18 months to germinate, and even then only a tiny percentage of the seeds is viable. Try stratifying the seeds by placing them in a container of 50/50 sand and peat mix and storing in a cool, mouse-free environment until February when they can be sown in the garden. It will be another two years before they are ready for transplanting. If you have room, try growing two or three together, hedge-fashion, to provide nest sites for hedge sparrow and chaffinch, and many species will enjoy the cover and will feed on the insects that live there.

A bonus from planting hawthorns will be the eventual arrival of some moths which, apart from their intrinsic interest, have larvae enjoyed by birds. Lackey, lappet, magpie, large thorn, mottled umber and swallow-tailed moth are but a few of the many species to be found on hawthorn, and these little forms of life add much interest to our contact with wildlife.

Crataegus laevigata. Midland Hawthorn

Less common, less thorny and not so tall in growth, it tends to grow more in the midlands and north. It flowers much earlier than the common hawthorn and thrives in shaded woodlands. Propagation is similar to the previous species and it is equally popular with the birds, whilst its soil preference is widely varied.

There are a few hybrid hawthorns on sale in nurseries but the present writer has had no experience with them so the advice given is to stick to the wild species. The heady perfume of the flowers will delight you in May and June and the berries will be welcomed by the birds in winter, especially blackbirds, fieldfares, song thrush and redwing when snow covers the ground.

Crataegus prunifolia. Ornamental Thorn

This much smaller thorn produces large red haws quite late into winter. It will grow into a large shrub or, if you prefer, small tree with a height over four metres and a similar spread. It likes an open, sunny position, is hardy and, with clustered white flowers in June followed by colourful autumn foliage, makes an attractive addition to both your garden and the habitat you are trying to create. If you buy a container-grown specimen, it will take a while to recover after planting.

Escallonia 'Donard seedling'

This is a shrub that makes a wonderful hedge, fairly quick growing and when well established provides ideal cover for the birds. Its evergreen leaves form a barrier to the winds, whilst within their cover a well-formed network of small branches makes good nest sites for many small birds. Blackbirds in particular favour escallonia. If your garden is near the sea, this bush will do well and, whilst apparently thriving on salty winds and sea spray, will protect the rest of the garden from the cold winter wind force. Some garden books say it needs protection from winds, but certainly on the south-west coast it defies even the east winds.

There are many cultivated varieties, but some are less hardy, so keep to escallonia 'Donard seedling'. It will grow quickly up to 2.5 metres and responds to trimming by renewing leaf growth in record time. As a summer bonus it produces massed pinkish-red flowers and its new succulent shoots bear aromatic leaves. With so many attractive features, we can forgive the fact that its seeds are neglected by the birds. Propagate by semi-hard cuttings in September or purchase container-grown shrubs from a nursery.

Fagus sylvatica. Beech

The capacity of this tree for bearing a crop of nuts varies tremendously according to the season. As I write, we have just experienced two hot summers followed by mild winters and the beeches are laden down with the golden-brown nuts. Although it is August, they will not be ready for many more weeks.

Due to its height potential and the dense shade cast by its thick foliage, this is not a tree for the small garden. Nevertheless it is a bearer of rich crops of beech nuts which are much loved by birds, so most bird gardeners will prefer to visit the nearest wild trees during September and October and collect a bagful to offer on the bird table.

On calcareous soils in spring, in frost-free areas protected from high, cold winds, a small beech may grow to two metres in height within two years. An excellent tree for the birds and the patient, understanding gardener, it should be planted with a view to the future, but nevertheless is most rewarding as it grows.

Hedera helix. Ivy

Bird gardening is one of those hobbies that contradicts most horticultural principles. Hence ivy, often regarded as a pest, is a boon to those of us trying to encourage birds. It makes good cover, especially low down, even flourishing as a cascading greenery from tree trunks or walls, and being evergreen it provides much-needed dry shelter in winter. If you happen to have a hedge bank then an ivy planted on top of it will soon spread downwards (as well as upwards) and provide those areas of shaded protection beloved by wrens, for its recesses harbour numerous spiders, harvestmen, woodlice and small insects that wrens feed on throughout the year. Despite the bad press it has had in the past, it does little damage to trees.

Often I have watched sparrows or a dunnock moving through the loose shaded structure, and migratory blackcaps seem to favour it. One blackcap (presumably the same one) came at about the same time for four consecutive years.

Ivy, like all green and growing plants, helps to clothe man-made structures, to soften their edges and outlines and thus make them more attractive to the birds. Old buildings, like old trees, are often embraced by this climber and nearly always you will hear and see birds among the firm and glossy leaves. Find room for an ivy plant and you will find room for birds.

Ilex aquifolium. Holly

As much a part of Christmas as the robin, the holly tree will provide decoration for the festive season, and the cutting of its branches will ensure a richer crop of berries next year. It responds to such pruning, and your garden blackbird will certainly relish the berries. Indeed, once a blackbird starts on your tree, it is remarkable how quickly it will clear it. I well remember once when we put a number of berried branches in a bucket of water out in the garden, several days before Christmas. When we came to arrange it with the decorations, every single berry had been eaten—proof of its bird popularity, and since it was Christmas we were delighted that they had enjoyed their pre-Christmas dinner.

Opposite: *Bird gardeners are fortunate in being able to plant those trees and bushes which will bear a rich harvest of luscious fruits and berries. Some of the most popular are (reading downwards): dog rose, guelder rose, ivy, hawthorn, elder, sloe, holly, blackberry, wild cherry, rowan, blackcurrant. Berries for the birds and wonderful colour for the autumn garden.*

Remember, however, that it is only the female tree that produces the berries, and since usually all the flowers on a single tree are of the same sex, you will need a nearby male to ensure regular cropping. Check with the nursery and sex your trees before leaving, and so avoid disappointment. The male is essential, if less spectacular, but it is the female berry-producer the birds will thrive on. However, hermaphrodite trees are often sold by nurseries so in limited space this may be a good compromise.

Redwings relish holly berries in hard seasons and I recall an observation that underlined this. In a south-west valley woodland nature reserve there is a large area beneath the oaks where many holly bushes are growing. The warden informed me they were the result of redwings roosting in the oaks after feeding on the berries from mature hollies elsewhere. Propagation can be by stratified seeds (18–24 months) or cuttings about ten centimetres long taken with a heel. Both seeds and cuttings should be kept in a cold frame for the first year of growth.

Laurus nobilis.   Sweet Bay or Poet's Laurel
There is a double bonus if you plant this evergreen shrub, because its berries are appreciated by birds and its aromatic leaves can be used to garnish fish dishes. A good specimen will grow to three or four metres with a spread of two-and-a-half to three metres, and its small glossy leaves form good cover for birds. Unfortunately, being a Mediterranean species, its leaves are often seared by cold winds, but in a sheltered, sunny situation it will thrive. It is unisexual, each shrub producing either all male or all female flowers, and the one you want for the bird garden is of course the female, to produce the berries. Both male and female plants produce inconspicuous greenish-yellow flowers in April and the shiny black berries are ripe from the end of October into early December.

Cuttings of lateral shoots—with a heel—should be inserted into a mix of equal parts sand and peat and allowed to form roots. In early May you can pot them up in John Innes No 1 and leave to develop for a year. If a friend has a mature shrub in the garden, you could layer one or two shoots in late summer and then separate them and replant next year. But remember to choose a female plant.

A few years ago a gardening friend brought me some shiny black berries about the size of a cherry stone, which she had found on the path at the side of her house. Despite searching, no tree producing such berries appeared to be growing in the vicinity. Then, quite unexpectedly, this November I noticed the path at the side of our house was littered with 'nuts' (yes, they were about the size of cherry stones!). Amongst them were a few of the black berries similar to those my friend had found. Then quite suddenly the penny dropped! Immediately above was the TV aerial on which starlings gathered regularly. The connection between the seeds and the birds seemed almost complete. So I sent the observation off to Dr David Snow, author of *Birds and Berries*. He informed me that the seeds were sweet bay and that they were probably eaten by the starlings for the pulp coating which contained up to 54 per cent fat. The 'nuts' are probably poisonous and so, after digesting the pulp, the 'nuts' are regurgitated—in our garden, by the starlings. Blackbirds seem to enjoy them as well.

Lonicera.   Honeysuckle

A June evening with bird song and the heady perfume of honeysuckle is so typical of our countryside that it simply must be included in the bird garden.

It is a flower that not only attracts the beautiful hawk moths, but has an amazing flowering sequence. Early in the evening its flower buds stand upright in such a position that it cannot self-pollinate itself. Then as the evening passes on, these flowers open out, usually about three to four hours before dusk. Now they bend downwards into a horizontal position and release a wonderfully strong aromatic scent.

Hawk moths fly in on the waves of perfume and insert their long, delicate tongues deep into the flower. So by next morning the flower is pollinated and changes in colour as its white deepens to a pale yellow. Nothing to do with birds, of course, but a fascinating addition to any bird garden.

Honeysuckle thrives with a cool root run and grows well in partial shade—hence its frequent association with hazel coppice in open deciduous woodland. The wild honeysuckle, *Lonicera periclymenum*, is a fairly fast grower and should be planted where it can scramble into the lower branches of a rowan or silver birch, or indeed *any* tree. It will thrive on a sheltered fence or ramble through a shrub and help to beautify the wall of the garden shed. If it is kept healthy by occasional pruning and by removing some of the older wood, it will in time provide the sort of tangled undergrowth, covered shade and wind protection that birds so often seek.

There are many forms of honeysuckle on sale at garden centres, all with very attractive flowers, so if you prefer to plant one of these, first check that it is a vigorous grower, to provide what the birds need, as well as a delight for the eye.

Honeysuckle can be propagated by cuttings 15–23 cm long and kept in a cold frame.

Prunus avium.   Wild Cherry or Gean

A tree for large gardens and one which will grow up to 20 metres, bearing very attractive snow-white flowers in April. The fruits are three to five in a bunch, glossy yellow in colour turning to bright red, but these are eaten by birds before turning to their ripe blackish-red.

Prunus padus.   Bird Cherry

Because it grows to a height of nine metres, this is not a tree for the small garden. Its white flowers are borne on pendent stems late in May. Black fruit follows and ripens during July. A deciduous tree, the green leaves change through shades of yellow to bright red until the first gales of autumn sweep them off the tree in October.

The fruits are eaten by mistle thrush, song thrush and blackbird. Carrion crows, which do occasionally visit gardens, have a rich and varied diet, and part of it consists of cherries. Jays, whose main autumn diet is acorns, will also feed on cherries. In the event of being unable to find a container-grown specimen, the bird cherry can easily be grown from seed. Use ripe ones and, having removed most of the flesh, make the 'stones' as clean as possible under the tap. Bury in damp sand and leave in a cold frame most of the winter, well protected from voles and mice, then sow them in the garden in early spring. It will be two years before you can transplant them as small trees.

Prunus spinosa.   Blackthorn (Sloe)
If you have a spacious garden, this is a good plant for an untidy corner. A single rooted cutting will, in the course of a few years, produce a series of suckers which will move outwards to colonise and soon produce a thicket of impenetrable, thorny density. It is ideal cover for birds and a frequent site for the nests of blackbirds and thrushes, but not, repeat *not*, for the small garden. However, if kept under control by constantly removing the suckers, you will enjoy the white flowers frosting the black stems in early March. A song thrush may then feed on the sloes in the following December or January. You might also enjoy some home-made sloe gin to warm the 'cockles of your heart' on a winter's evening, as you look forward to next season's nest among the dagger-like thorns.

Pyracantha coccinea.   Firethorn
There are some ten species of pyracantha and this one is the most attractive to birds. It is an evergreen shrub, ideal for growing against a wall or as a hedging plant and will go to three or four metres tall. If it is kept well pruned it produces massed bright red berries in late summer, but you need only cut back the current year's growth to half-way. A bonus is the pretty white hawthorn-like flowers in June. If you train it up some stout trellis-work against a wall, its spiny branches and sheltering leaves may well provide a nest site for your garden blackbird, who will also enjoy the persistent berries long after its fledglings have flown.

Pyracantha rogersiana
Another extremely popular bush with birds, and its orange-red berries growing in clusters follow the white flowers that bloom in June. It will grow to a height of over two metres. Like many other bird bushes, it can be bought at garden centres in a pot and should be planted out between the end of September and March.

Rosa canina.   Dog Rose
A native beauty, so often taken for granted because it is so familiar, yet capable of charming the gardener and welcoming the birds, the wild briar is common in our hedgerows where its white to pale pink flowers delight the eye in the month of June. The egg-shaped hips that result spatter the same hedges with blood-red in autumn and in some years the hips remain throughout early winter. Much enjoyed by fieldfares and blackbirds, they are also attractive to hawfinches and greenfinches. As a climber it will need controlling, unless you are able to plant it in a semi-natural hedge or wild corner. Be prepared for it to grow to a height of two or more metres. Its strong arching stems, well armed with hooked prickles, easily bear the weight of small birds. Dog roses prefer sunlight and if growing in the shade often fail to flower. It can be kept well pruned in a hedge situation where it will form a dense, impenetrable barrier.

The song thrush is usually regarded as a snail eater, yet earthworms, slugs, a few other invertebrates together with fruits and berries also form part of its diet. The firethorn (Pyracantha rogersiana) is eaten by blackbirds and may attract a hungry winter fieldfare.

It is a plant very easily propagated from hardwood cuttings taken in the autumn, preferably late September.

Find a plant growing in the wild and select shoots about 25 cm long from the current year's growth, on which the thorns break off cleanly. Cut the shoot a couple of centimetres above its joint with the main stem. Cut off the thin tip, remove all leaves and thorns from the bottom 15 cm and insert the cutting some 15 cm into a well sanded shallow trench, making sure you thoroughly firm the soil around it. Within a year it should have developed a good root system and will be ready for planting out.

Rosa arvensis. Field Rose
A similar climbing wild rose, flowering in July and August—a little later than the

previous species—and bearing creamy white flowers smaller than the more common dog rose. This plant will grow to two metres in height if well supported, for example by hawthorns. Otherwise it tends to sprawl and be of little consequent use to the bird gardener. The field rose tends to prefer deep or heavy clay soils providing they are well drained, whereas the dog rose will grow in a variety of soils providing they are neither too dry nor too wet.

The hips are smaller than those of the dog rose but propagation is identical.

These climbing wild roses deserve space in your garden from both an aesthetic and a food source viewpoint. They are easy to keep under control either by careful tying-in or gentle pruning, and since their hips remain on the stems well into the winter—if not already eaten—they provide a long-standing attraction for the birds.

Rubus fruticosus.   Bramble

Familiar in most hedgerows, wasteland and woodland edge, this is a sprawling bush that provides ideal food for the birds—and just the right flavouring for a blackberry and apple pudding, with clotted cream.

In large, wild gardens, the bramble will prove a winner for birds, but it does need space. Then its foliage and stems blend in with tall growing plants and grasses to form an attractive hide-out for many birds. It also helps to develop a habitat rich in other species, and that amalgam is what wildlife needs to flourish. Its great bonus is the berries which provide bird food from late August until early October.

Brambles can also be grown under controlled conditions. Trained along a wall or fence and kept well pruned, a plant will cover many square feet and provide plenty of fruit. Unfortunately, when grown in that manner its cover value is negligible. By careful searching on the edge of a bramble thicket you will soon spot some branch tips that have rooted. Simply cut them from the main plant, dig up the rooted tip with a trowel and replant where required in your own garden.

Sambucus nigra.   Common Elder

One slight problem with this bush is that some of the bushes produce flowers smelling of tom-cats' urine. Whereas the home wine-maker can smell the blooms before picking them, the bird gardener has to trust to luck when buying a specimen. However, fortunately this does not affect the berries and birds will always flock to them.

The elder is a vigorous growing bush that thrives on disturbed ground, so if you have a garden that at one time was used as a dump, perhaps for instance during the house building process, then that is *the* place to plant it. In my experience it is an ideal bush to plant on a bank or in the corner of your garden where it may grow freely, perhaps to a height of four metres, with a considerable spread as well. The great advantage of having an elder in such a position—preferably as far removed from the house as possible—is that it makes an ideal assembly point for birds. Birds arriving to feed often prefer to alight some distance from the bird table and survey the ground. Here they pause awhile, especially if they have happened to see you put out food, before descending to feed. Here, small parties of starlings will 'talk' to each other about matters one would dearly like to translate, before dispatching one of their number to scout out the prospects at the table. Greenfinches, too, flit down to the peanut bag, release one and fly back to cover before eating it.

Elder is a great provider of those black berries from August till the end of October, when song thrush and robin may visit it for food.

It is worth remembering that black and red are favourite berry colours with birds, possibly due to their conspicuous shades and the way birds see things.

The elder planted in your garden will be one of the first bushes to open its buds to late winter sunshine and so reminds us of better days to come when we can enjoy its dramatic flowers that richly scent the May evenings.

Sorbus aria. Whitebeam
This is another attractive foliage tree, with its wind-blown leaves flashing silver-white as they turn. It will grow to six metres and each autumn provide a russet and gold leaf display before they fall. For the birds its rich harvest of red fruits hang in bunches, ripe and ready in September. Plant during late autumn until early spring, and if you collect a few seeds you can sow them in any good seed compost and grow on for three or four years before finally placing in the bird garden. You will probably prefer to buy a large pot-grown specimen from the local garden centre.

The seeds are taken by some of the garden finches, and the spreading branches provide both good cover and perching places throughout the year. Since there are over a hundred species, ensure that your specimen is *S. aria*, the common white-beam, which is especially fond of chalk or limestone soils.

Sorbus aucuparia. Rowan, Mountain Ash
This small tree is ideal for the bird garden as its clusters of red berries are eagerly eaten by members of the thrush family. It prefers light soils and will grow in moorland at altitudes above any other tree. A newly planted tree may take up to three years to become fruit-bearing and only well established trees bear a worth-while crop. In the wild I have watched flocks of fieldfares descend on a rowan, each bird consuming a large quantity of ripened berries before departing, to return again, having remembered the rich food source. In our garden a small rowan bears only some thirty berry clusters and here in late August, after the berries have turned from yellow to orange and then red, our local starlings set to work and strip the tree in a single day.

Propagation can be from seed. Collect a few fruits when almost ripe and store them in a sealed polythene bag. Leave until thoroughly ripe—or better still, until rotting. Squash out the seeds and wash thoroughly in water. When clean, sow them in boxes with some sort of protection from mice and birds. Be patient, for the seeds will lie dormant for many months before germinating.

Container-grown trees are available from nurseries, but choose a plant under 1.5 metres in height, with a strong, straight stem. After some ten or more years, it will have grown to 4.5 metres in height, with a spread of nearly three metres, and will produce a great crop of berries.

In general it will be the rowans in upland gardens, farmland and really rural areas that are visited by the birds. In lowland gardens it is more likely to offer food to song thrush, mistle thrush, blackbird and starlings.

Taxus baccata.   Yew
If you keep pets it is wiser to forgo the attraction of its berries which, whilst containing poisonous seeds, are avidly consumed by birds without their coming to any harm. The foliage and bark are also poisonous, containing taxine. But despite its dangers, the berries are much sought after by greenfinches and mistle thrush when they ripen during August, turning red by September. So the decision is left to you.

Normally the yew produces male and female flowers on separate trees. The male flowers are found on the underside of shoots whereas female flowers grow out from very small buds on the end of the shoots. As the female flower matures it secretes a sticky substance to which male pollen adheres, resulting eventually in a large seed covered by a juicy skin which, as it ripens, turns from green to pale red.

A few yew trees go against the general rule and produce both male and female flowers on the same tree. For the birds you need the berries, so a female tree or one of the bi-sexual ones will be required.

This common churchyard tree once provided wood for long-bows, and many of these ancient trees are over one thousand years old. Plant a yew and you plant for posterity.

Viburnum opulus.   Guelder Rose
This beautiful flowering shrub or small tree is not a member of the rose family but belongs to the honeysuckle family along with elder, wayfaring tree and snow-berry. It will grow to more than four metres and attain a spread of over three.

It has flat heads of white, heavily scented flowers which in appearance resemble the flower heads of the elder. It flowers in May but the real bonus is its translucent red berries which are frequently eaten by blackbirds, mistle thrush and fieldfare.

If you have a damp garden this is a shrub well worth planting; in the wild it is found growing in damp woods, close to streams and in the fens.

TREES AND SHRUBS AS ROOSTING PLACES

As far as birds are concerned, there is a bonus in any well planted garden that has abundant cover. As evening draws in, birds go to roost and each species goes about preparation for the night's rest in its own way. Outside the breeding season many birds seek out communal sites where varying numbers will gather together to sleep. Perhaps the best known example is the starlings which gather together in small parties late in a winter's afternoon, perhaps on your roof, and fly up to join an ever-growing flock of their fellows to fly to the roost. This is often—as in London—on tall buildings or, in the country, in a clump of tall trees or quite often in reed beds. That's where your garden starlings may sleep at night.

Table 1. Berry and fruit seasons, and flowering periods.

FOOD PLANT	Jan	Feb	Mar	April	May	June	July	Aug	Sept	Oct	Nov	Dec
Amelanchier laevis				0000		<------	---->					
Cotoneaster 'Cornubia'	<------	------>				0000		<------	-----	------	------	----->
Cotoneaster horizontalis						0000	<---	------>				
Crataegus monogyna	<------	------>			0000	0000			<------	------	------	----->
Crataegus prunifolia	<----->					0000		<-----	------	------	------	----->
Fagus sylvatica					0000				<------	------>		
Hedera helix						<//////////>			0000	0000	0000	
Ilex aquifolium					0000	0000	0000	0000		<------	------	----->
Lonicera							0000	<--	----->	0000	<---	----->
Prunus padus					0000		<----	------	---->			
Prunus spinosa			0000						<------	------	----->	
Pyracantha coccinea	<----->					0000	0000		<---	------	------	----->
Pyracantha rogersiana						0000	0000		<---	------	------	----->
Rosa arvensis						0000	0000		<------	----->		
Rosa canina						0000	0000		<------	----->		
Rubus fruticosus						0000	0000	<-	------	----->		
Sambucus nigra						0000		<----->				
Sorbus aria						0000	<------	----->				
Sorbus aucuparia					0000	0000	<------	----->				
Taxus baccata			0000	0000					<---	----->		
Viburnum opulus					0000	0000			<------	------	------>	

oooo   denotes flowering period
<----›   denotes berries available
<///›   denotes berries ripe following year

These seasons are only approximate and will vary between north and south regions and also according to weather conditions prevailing before and after flowering. In some instances the berries will be consumed by the birds well before the end of the season indicated.

During the breeding season many of our finches roost singly or in pairs, but as autumn arrives they gather in ever enlarging flocks to sleep in clumps of scrub, rhododendron or conifer. However, whereas chaffinches and linnets roost in many hundreds, goldfinches and bullfinches frequently sleep fewer than ten together. There are frequent reports of wrens sharing a common roost in a hollow tree or maybe a large nest box.

But many of our garden birds, especially the blackbird, sometimes roost alone, and this is where the thoughtful bird gardener can provide much-needed cover. Thick evergreen bushes such as escallonia provide ideal cover against the cold winter sea winds; thick clumps of ivy are often sought out by sparrows in summer, but in winter they congregate in their large warm nests of the previous season.

Whatever species and wherever they are, a common urge dominates their behaviour—the need to find a protected site where the wind force is broken, a place safe from the hardest frost or sheltered from rain and, most importantly, safe from predators. In winter the limited fat reserves of all our birds dwindle rapidly and in very adverse conditions much of each day is spent in replenishing energy lost during the cold, dark hours.

Try to plan the garden so that such features are either against, or protected by, a wall well sheltered from the prevailing wind. In general a south-facing place is best: not only does this save a roosting bird from wind force, but it gathers in whatever modicum of sun's heat may be available. By careful observation around the garden you should also be able to determine the drier areas, another important factor in roosting.

The tit family are particularly prone to solitary roosting, and due to their small size they do need a dry place free from the cold. In the wild, hollow trees provide welcome shelter in winter, and such places may well prove to be their nest site in the ensuing spring.

In our gardens, the best we can offer are, for example, thick evergreen hedges, thick unpruned wall climbers, ivy patches, evergreen trees, nest boxes and piled brushwood against a fence or wall. In my own garden an open window in a small garden shed provided access for a small unidentified (because I wished to avoid disturbance) bird which regularly roosted on one of the roof joists. A pad of paper on the bench below caught the droppings and provided the visiting card whereby I knew when my little guest had shared the welcome shelter.

White droppings on the soil or dropping-spotted twigs provide clues to a roosting site above, and such roosts can easily be found by careful searching in likely places around the garden.

Conifers for roosting

Conifers deserve a place in the bird garden on three counts: firstly, they provide safe, sheltered roosting places; secondly, they are attractive trees both in form and in colour; thirdly, some birds may be encouraged to visit your garden because they favour conifers. It is all part of the habitat recognition by birds.

Any nursery or garden centre will offer you a very wide range of species together with advice on cultural conditions, height and spread, but further care is needed in the selection of suitable species for birds. In the wild environment it is spruce, larch and pine that are the habitat of conifer-loving birds, but in the garden — certainly in the average one — they grow too large, so cultivated hybrids and other species are the answer.

The first matter to decide, therefore, is the height to which you would like your conifer to grow and then, armed with a good reference book, you can begin your search. One of the handiest is *The Tree and Shrub Expert* by Dr D. G. Hessayon, well illustrated in colour and providing all the details you need.

The specimen you buy will probably be container-grown or have its roots in a ball; this latter kind should be planted in late spring or early autumn.

For the bird garden roost you will need a semi- or fully spreading species, one with just a few small spaces in the foliage where birds can hop in. The tightly-knit columnar types are unsuitable, as are the very low growing dwarf types — beware cats and predators! Their height range is anywhere from 30 centimetres to 30 metres, but a growth of three metres attained in ten years should be the absolute maximum for a small garden. Some species are lime haters, others thrive on lime and others again dislike pollution. So check thoroughly before buying.

Abies.   Silver Fir
Abies koreana is ideal. It grows to about two metres in ten years, but being slow growing does not quickly provide roosting conditions.

Abies pinsapo, the Spanish fir, thrives on chalky soils and will give you a height of no more than 2.5 metres in ten years.

Cedrus.   Cedar
Blue-green *Cedrus atlantica* 'Glauca Pendula' will provide nest site and roost and be most picturesque growing to well over three metres in good conditions.

Chamaecyparis.   False Cypress
This conifer is most popular in garden centres and several varieties will be found, but many of them have upward-growing foliage sprays which are unsuitable for birds to enter. Choose wisely — perhaps *Chamaecyparis lawsoniana* 'Allumii'.

Picea.   Spruce
These will remind you of Christmas trees — and why not, for *Picea abies*, the common spruce, probably graces your Christmas decorations. A useful spruce growing to some two metres and with bluish-green leaves is *Picea brewerana*, one with a growing habit that makes it possible to hang peanuts from its upper branches.

Thuja.   'Arbor-vitae'
Of these, the best is western red cedar, *T. plicata*. Yes, I know it grows to six metres in ten years and has a wide spread, but the cover it offers to birds is first class. It is very easy to grow, too, so if you have a largish garden, why not try one?

Any overgrown corner will provide much-needed cover for the birds. Many small birds use these dark recesses as comfortable roosting sites. A pile of brushwood leant against a wall or a nest box draped with ivy may attract spring nesters. And clematis 'Nelly Moser' is a real bonus for the bird watcher.

As natural inhabitants of fir and conifer woods, goldcrests may be attracted by judicious planting of such trees. As occasional visitors to your garden they will feed on insects and spiders.

Conifers generally are slow growing, so you need to think ahead before you plant and try to visualise its more mature form in relation to the garden as a whole. Some conifers are quite expensive, but if regarded as an investment in bird gardening they will produce good feathered dividends.

Their only disadvantage is that since most of them are not indigenous species, it could be argued that they are not readily appreciated, nor do they form an easily assimilated habitat aspect to our birds. Against that, they are becoming so common in many gardens that the birds must be familiar with them, and both their scent and foliage appearance is probably close enough to wild species to prove attractive. I have certainly found sparrows, blackbird, blue tits, starlings, collared doves and chaffinches exploring some of them, especially in winter when

the deciduous shrubs have shed their covering leaves. Plant a suitable conifer and you provide a nesting site for a dunnock, whilst a chaffinch may use the tip of the tree as a singing post.

ATTRACTIVE PILLARS FOR PLANTS AND BIRDS

You can create a number of features that, apart from providing for the needs of the birds, will also add interest and beauty to your garden.

For example, one way to use ivy and at the same time provide nest sites is to start by building a brick pillar. Use attractive red house bricks or some of the artificial rock-types obtainable at DIY stores. If the pillar is being built in a lawn or similar soft area, you will need to dig a small foundation hole about 50 centimetres deep and some 10 to 15 centimetres wider than the pillar's base. Fill this with rubble and cement-mix or concrete. Construct the pillar using ordinary household mortar, but mix in a little colourant (obtainable from builder's merchants) to match the bricks or stonework. A tall pillar, say more than head height, should be at least two bricks' width on each side. The internal space between the bricks can be filled in with concrete up to the first metre in height and after that left hollow. A small flagstone can be used to seal the top and prevent rain entering.

Near the top and possibly on two sides fix nest boxes and allow the ivy to clamber all over them.

Ivy and clematis pillars

Your pillar can be planted with ivy as suggested, although a more floral display with abundant cover would be given by *Clematis montana*. Its twining leaf stalks will readily cling to either stretched wires, wire netting or trellis fixed to the pillar, and as it is a quick growing climber, it will soon cover whatever kind of support you offer it.

Clematis montana can be pruned quite severely after flowering and this helps to control its very vigorous growth. Should you want to increase your stock, perhaps to provide plants for other parts of the garden, take 15 cm half-ripened stem cuttings and put them in a fifty-fifty mixture of peat and rough sand. If you can provide modest bottom heat, this will encourage quick root-forming; if not, keep in a warmish situation free from wind. By early autumn pot on in John Innes No 1 and leave out in the garden until ready to plant the following autumn.

There are so many good, colourful climbing clematis, including some striking hybrids, that a list would not do justice to them. It is better to go along to a garden centre in the summer and choose the colour and form you prefer. But one cautionary word: many of them do not 'bush up' like *Clematis montana*, and this tried-and-tested flowering beauty really does deserve its place.

Opposite: Clockwise, from top left: *silver fir* (Abies koreana), *Norway spruce* (Picea abies), *and* Picea brewerana. *Conifers add variety to the bird garden, providing a safe refuge, a place to preen and a sheltered roost.* P. brewerana, *with its beautiful blue-green, shining foliage, is a visual delight for gardeners, too.*

Wigwam pillars

Another simple way to create a pillar is by using three pieces of wood in the form of a 'wigwam'. Three 2440 mm lengths of 50 x 50 or 75 x 50 rough-cut (that is, not planed), and treated with one of the preservatives—or preferably tanalised by the timber merchant—will form the outline. A small concrete foundation can have three pieces of drilled angle-iron or flat metal strips inserted into the wet concrete at a suitable angle and this will provide points of attachment for the wood. This keeps the wood clear of the wet ground and is better than sinking it into the concrete, which would inevitably lead to early rotting. At the point where the poles cross, fasten them together with galvanised wire, or nails if you prefer.

Plant this pyramid with summer jasmine (*Jasminum officinale* 'Grandiflorum') and clematis (*viticella* 'Purpurea Plena Elegans'), obtainable as container-grown plants around 90 to 120 centimetres tall. As they begin to grow tie them in lightly onto the posts, in a criss-cross pattern, and within two years or so you will have a beautiful mass of white and purple flowers in July and August and a possible nest site for birds in the spring. An added bonus would be to fix a nest box near the top, and whilst this might not be occupied until the climbers clamber over it, the birds would have had plenty of time to become accustomed to it.

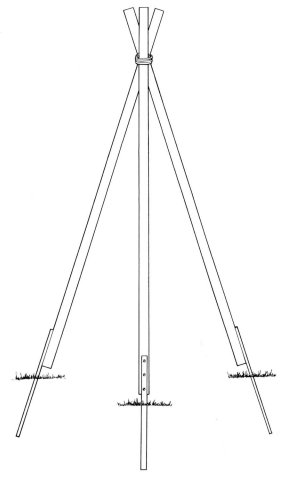

A wigwam pillar is easy to construct and can be made from processed timber or rustic poles. Metal feet, driven into the ground, will last longer than wood which inevitably rots at ground level.

Wild flowering climbers such as traveller's joy (Clematis vitalba) *and honeysuckle* (Lonicera periclymenum) *grow well together if planted at the base of the 'wigwam' and trained up the poles. In a few years you have a garden feature to be enjoyed by yourself and the birds. This blackbird has even built its nest in the thick, colourful cover.*

Old Man's Beard thicket

Almost everywhere you wander over limestone and chalk soil you will find the wild clematis (*Clematis vitalba*) hanging in loose festoons from the lower branches of oak and smaller shrubs and trees. A summer-flowering plant, known as Traveller's Joy, it produces masses of seed heads whose feathery white plumes give it its other name, Old Man's Beard.

It can have a twofold function in the bird garden. Firstly, it is a fast growing and very vigorous climber whose leafstalks twine around any object touched and is therefore useful if you want to obtain quick results on a pillar, a post or even a tree. Secondly, it quickly develops a loose, leafy entanglement which in summer provides cover for the birds. Like so many of our native wild plants it is an easily recognised species by passing birds, and as such provides encouragement to stay awhile and even seek a nesting place.

It is not commonly found in nurseries, so you should collect ripe seed from the wild in early autumn and sow into a good compost. Prick out seedlings into 75 or 100 mm pots provided with a 45 cm high stick for the plant to cling to. Tie in lightly and by the following autumn plant it out *in situ*. But keep an eye on its growth as it shoots up a tree and you may well need long-handled cutters to keep it under control.

I am quite convinced that birds visit places they recognise from a habitat mixture of plants, and in so doing scent and appearance of individual species play an important part. Recognition quickly relaxes a bird. Watch how birds alight on a certain branch or tree to return again and again, following what is almost a routine. Certainly there is more to a bird than most of us will ever realise and site recognition is something worth studying.

Hazel and honeysuckle

Hazel coppice with honeysuckle is another combination met with in the wild. Providing you have room in your garden, plant a hazel bush (*Corylus avellana*). After three or four years it will have grown to 120 or 150 cm in height, so then would be the time to drive a wooden stake, about 240 cm in length, well into the soil and fairly close to the main stem of the hazel. Close to this plant some honeysuckle—the wild one, *Lonicera periclymenum*. Select a good, strong-growing container specimen, and tie some of the stems to the post and one or two to branches of the hazel. Providing you are patient for a couple of years, you will be able to tie it in as it grows and very soon you will have a good tangled growth. It is not quite a pillar, perhaps, but it is good bird cover.

In a more formal garden climbers can be trained over arches, but since arches usually straddle paths, the resultant disturbance of passers-by can prove a deterrent. It is certainly no place for a nest box.

Whilst the reproduction of a small wild habitat is for the really keen bird person, many will probably want to add a few items, either plants or structural, to improve the bird potential of their existing gardens.

There is absolutely no conflict here. You could, for instance, easily add one or two of the suggested berry bushes, and if there is no room, why not root out a plant that has become bedraggled, or be bold and make a sacrifice for greater gain? Too often, as gardeners, we keep a tree, bush or herbaceous perennial long after its useful life has passed. After all, every plant has a limited life duration.

One herbaceous perennial that is also good for birds is the Michaelmas daisy (*Aster* spp), and it will give you flowering beauty whilst providing food for finches later in the year. *Aster novae-angliae* and *A. novi-belgii* are two Michaelmas daisies that flower profusely and grow to more than 90 cm in height.

In our garden, some years ago, we planted seven Michaelmas daisy plants in a small border surrounded by African marigolds. Up to that time we had never been visited by goldfinches, so you can imagine our pleasure when a 'charm' of seven arrived on a sunny autumn morning and fed hungrily. And what's more they returned several times, until a stormy spell finally disposed of any seeds remaining. A little earlier that year, just before the summer blooms of the marigolds began to fade, dozens of silver Y moths came every dusk to suck the nectar. They are a 'tame' species and one can go very close to them as they feed, their wings trembling as they walk among the petals.

Although it is most frequently used in sponsored charity causes to see who can raise the tallest, the sunflower is well worth its place. In a good summer, if you have planted four to six of them against a wall or hedge, their heads will hold a rich crop of large seeds. I know you can buy the seeds included in mixtures for wild birds, but it is much more satisfying to watch blue and great tits busy on the large flat heads. Greenfinches, too, should find them as they wander past in the search for food. By early autumn the dinner-plate sized seed heads should be ripe. The best plan then is to cut them off during a dry spell of weather and hang them in the garden shed or similar dry and airy place. One cold winter day you can hang the seed head from a tree branch and let the birds feed freely.

ONE FOR YOU AND ONE FOR THE BIRDS

Bird gardening at its simplest is the planting of a plant that will be enjoyed by the birds whilst giving you the satisfaction of watching them feed where none fed before. It can be a very worthwhile reward.

But, of course, decisions have to be taken and choices made, especially where fruits are concerned. Even if you want to grow fruits for household needs it is still possible to protect your blackcurrant bushes and yet leave one for the birds. Your garden blackbird will enjoy them, but bear in mind that those protecting nets can prove a hazard.

One of the most popular garden fruit trees is the apple and without stipulating any particular variety, you might like to consider planting one. Take some of the fruit for your own use and leave the rest on the tree. The birds will know exactly when they are ripe, usually in October, and will begin to feed on them. Flocks of starlings enjoy the fruit and one day some of the apples will drop. Leave them where they fall, for on the ground they offer another bonus not only for ground-feeding birds but for butterflies as well. In the autumn sunshine the last of the

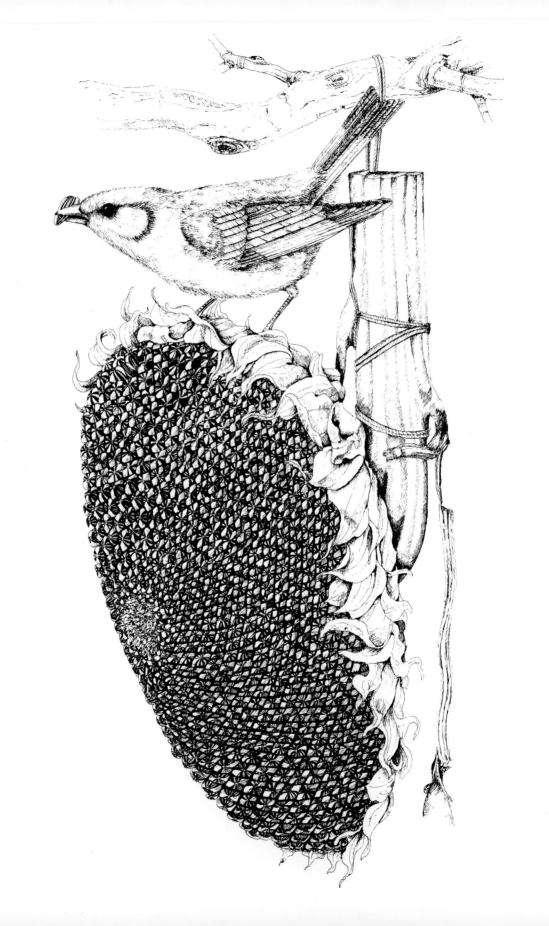

summer butterflies will fly in. Red admirals, peacocks and tortoiseshell alight on the fruit and their delicate tongues dip down into the drops of sugar-sweet fruit juice in the peck-holes left by the birds. For many this will be their last meal before hibernating, for others their last sweet nectar drink before autumn's first frost numbs and stills their fragile bodies. Perhaps, if you have room, you might like to store a few summer fruits and then when the snow arrives put out an apple or pear or even a plum if you can spare it, and the winter migrants like fieldfare and redwing may find food where little else is available.

Any fruit, in fact, can be left on the ground, for there will be some creature that will enjoy it. Even the little fieldmouse chews away at fallen apples and many a Beauty of Bath or Cox's will bear its teeth-marks, so often mistaken for the beak marks of a bird.

Dear, oh dear, what would a horticultural adviser have to say about such negligent gardening—especially when every gardening book and media programme goes to great lengths to persuade you to rake up, clear out those slug-lurking spots and pick the fruit with such care and attention!

Whilst on the subject of clearing up, think about all those fallen leaves covering the lawn. You might consider leaving them for a week or two longer, just so that the worms can have a feed.

And what an enormous amount of life lives on, in and below the grass of the lawn. Just take as an example a lawn measuring about 14 x 6 metres—that is, 84 square metres in area—and consider the following facts harvested from George Ordish's book *The Living Garden*. By converting his figures to suit a lawn of 84 square metres, we find in the top 23 cm of soil on that lawn around 558 earthworms. Think what that represents in terms of food for birds, especially if we resist any temptation to spray chemicals on it. In addition there may be a million miles of fungal mycelium—yes one million miles—as well as astronomical numbers of bacteria and protozoa, the former being eaten by the latter. Then there are eelworms from 0.5–1.5 mm long and small 'pot worms' (Enchytraeidae) numbering hundreds of thousands. Along with all these are the mites, springtails, fly larvae, beetle larvae and spiders. Yet as we walk on the lawn all we see are the worm casts, and in late summer the crane flies or daddy-long-legs with their 64 mm wingspan, and perhaps in summer a swarm of tiny 'gnats' rising and falling in the still air, each one with a wingspan of less than 1.5 mm, all of which have spent part of their life history beneath the lawn.

So, a good bird lawn will be one wherein all this wealth of wildlife is encouraged. And how best to do that? Well, once more the keen bird gardener will fly in the face of modern horticultural practice! Firstly, having mown the lawn, leave the mown cuttings on the grass; next time you can brush them away; the time after that leave them, and so on. This will give the worms time to come out at night and feed on both lawn mowings and fallen leaves. Better-fed worms means more

Opposite: *Ripe sunflower seed heads act like a magnet to greenfinches. The young birds first learn to feed on small seeds, usually weeds, but by the arrival of autumn they have 'graduated' to larger seeds and sunflowers seeds are particularly enjoyed.*

worms and that in turn provides better winter and spring food for our birds.

At the same time those worms are adding humus to your lawn which will help keep it moist and green next summer, and even if the early bird does catch the worm there will be plenty left. Come mid-November you could rake up the fallen leaves and compost them or even spread them beneath the hedges and bushes to provide a breeding environment for the multitude of small invertebrates beloved of birds.

Incidentally, if you have a compost heap, turn it occasionally during the winter by forking a small portion of the surface to reveal a few more worms and invertebrates. As your local robin and blackbird become familiar with this food release they will fly in to feed as you walk away. Compost is an all-round 'greener' for your garden and its beneficial effects on your plants will amaze you. And the birds certainly benefit.

But what about all those pests, did I hear you say? Well, pests are simply those creatures that affect *our* interests and not, repeat not, those of the birds, for they thrive on all those 'baddies' we try to obliterate with death-dealing methods. I firmly believe that every bird gardener should completely forgo the use of chemical sprays and applications, and even when buying 'safe' preparations the formula should be *very* carefully read. Unfortunately for wildlife, our record in the use of chemicals is studded with errors and mistakes, and although attitudes have changed it is still possible to find those dangerous ones on sale.

Generally speaking, birds flourish on what we term 'pests' and you only have to spend an hour in an uncontaminated woodland to appreciate the multitude of bird life. There, among the vegetation, live countless insects, some with exploding populations, others with stable ones, yet over a prolonged period of time they balance out. Go green and ban the sprays.

3
WILD PLANTS FOR GARDEN BIRDS

For the bird gardener the small wild plants are as valuable an acquisition as trees and shrubs. Most gardeners call them weeds but perhaps the best definition of a weed is 'a plant growing where it is not wanted'. For the birds, however, a few of those weeds are very attractive and no bird garden should be without them. Try and find a small patch of ground where you can plant out a few.

There is a problem which always arises whenever 'weeds' are encouraged: *they thrive and spread*, so there is need for care or you will find them taking over your herbaceous border. Whilst an untidy garden may encourage the birds, for most gardeners there is a constant pull between freedom and control.

Let us assume that, within reason, you intend to give birds priority. To gain some experience in the 'wild weed' field, spend a little while, in late summer or early autumn, bird-watching on waste-ground or a rough uncultivated place. There you will find flocks of mixed finches feeding on a number of seed-bearers, many of almost insignificant size—hardheads, ragwort, groundsel, dandelion, chickweed, dog's mercury, charlock, persicaria and wild radish. By simply watching what the birds are eating and then identifying the plants, you will have gained an invaluable insight into the birds' habits. And later you will be able to offer some of those wild habitat foods in your own garden, with the certainty that the birds like them.

One plant very attractive to birds and quite easily grown from seeds collected in the wild is the spear thistle (*Cirsium vulgare*) and such seeds can be collected in late summer. Using a small plastic container or a seed box filled with any good moistened compost, sprinkle a few seeds on the surface and cover with a dusting of compost. Place the container in a sealed polythene bag under the staging in your greenhouse or any protected part of your garden. As soon as the seedling thistles crowd the box, transplant them into the garden. If you prefer you can sow the seed directly into the garden, but the former method has much to commend it. All the ensuing care they need is the same as for any other plant.

It is really satisfying when, in the following year, a charm of goldfinches arrive to feed. They have come simply and solely because you provided the food they needed and for which they were searching.

As the season moves on, many of the seeds will have collected in bushes or fallen to the ground and some will remain attached to the parent plant. Another good bird plant, not quite so easy to find although it is widespread in rough grassy places, is the teasel (*Dipsacus fullonum*), a handsome wild plant growing to a height of 90 cm and producing the familiar conical and prickly flowerheads that have a pale purple hue in summer, while later in autumn and winter the prickly stems and stiff flowerheads turn an attractive pale golden colour. It is a pretty plant that will add beauty to your wild patch in winter and has the added advantage

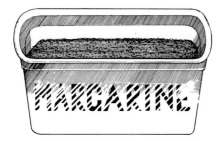

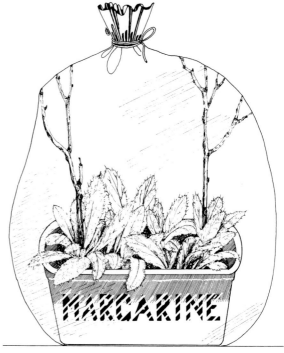

Spear thistle (Cirsium vulgare) *seeds are easy to grow into an excellent food plant. Collect seeds from a wild plant, sow on surface of compost in a plastic container and cover* very lightly. *Dampen compost and cover with polythene bag. Transplant seedlings into garden.*

that it provides seeds for wandering goldfinches. If you decide to collect the seeds, wait until early autumn, but remember, the birds may have been there first.

Another prickly plant is the burdock (*Arctium minus*)—the sticky buds of childhood, that children delight in throwing at each other so that the marble-sized flowerheads stick to the clothes. The seeds of this plant, when they ripen during the winter, are sought by greenfinches and goldfinches. It forms a very large plant so is not recommended if you have only limited space.

Bristly ox-tongue (*Picris echioides*) grows to a height of nearly 90 cm with spreading stems thickly armed with prickles. In June and early July it produces many pale yellow dandelion-like flowers in groups of five or six clustered together. The seeds number an average fifty per head, and since a single plant may have over one hundred and fifty seed heads, it may carry well over seven thousand seeds. Those not eaten on the plant fall to the ground or are carried some distance away to form a winter food source.

A plant with spine-toothed leaves, growing to more than 60 cm and bearing numerous small dandelion-like flowers, is the prickly sowthistle (*Sonchus asper*). It produces parachute seeds in July which will spread around your garden, unless previously eaten. If you have keen horticultural neighbours close by it might be diplomatic to forgo this species. Closely related and with similar flowers is the common sowthistle (*Sonchus oleraceus*), a prolific seed-maker visited by wandering bands of goldfinches in late summer, not a particularly pretty plant for the bird garden but nevertheless a useful additional food source in the wild patch.

In complete contrast to the sowthistles is a low-growing plant, despised as a persistent weed, yet one wonders why some plant breeder has not worked on it—the dandelion (*Taraxacum officinale*). Look into the golden-yellow disc of a dandelion in early summer, look really closely, and sunlight itself seems to glow among its petals. Yes, it does seed very freely and will colonise new soil, but those seeds are enjoyed by many finches, especially the greenfinch. Simply by growing dandelions you will not of course bring birds into your garden, but a truly natural habitat contains a rich variety of plants, and each is a small link with all the life that shares our garden with us. Every small link strengthens the chain of life between the wild environment and your created habitat and dandelions more than deserve their space. The seed heads, apart from their utilitarian use as a bird food source, are quite beautiful when viewed under a hand lens, so you get floral beauty, bird food and delicate structure, all to enjoy from the humble dandelion. And, there is an added bonus: the leaves can be used to flavour a salad by chopping a *few* and sprinkling them over the lettuce. If you cover a plant with a pot for a few days, the leaves will blanch and this makes them less bitter and a little more tender. Grown in your own garden they should be free from traffic exhaust and farm sprays—and next year they will still produce seeds for the birds.

Whilst dandelions glow along the roadsides, there is another flowering plant that colours entire fields in the warm summer days. It is a member of the cabbage family and called charlock or wild mustard (*Sinapis arvensis*). How pleasant the sight of a distant field flashing yellow in the May and June sunlight, unbroken colour from thousands of flowerheads of this once so common weed of the corn-fields; a delightful miniature in a green and painted landscape. It is a prolific bearer of seeds, with each of the multitude of pod-like fruits sheltering up to a dozen seeds. Not that you can provide garden room for a display that graces many a farm, but sow a few seeds to multiply into late summer bird food. A countryman's plant that indicates land free from selective weedkillers, long may it bloom in our May and June countryside or add a flash of colour to the bird garden.

A much 'tidier' wild flower regularly visited by birds is knapweed or hardheads (*Centaurea nigra*). This perennial with its purple or bluish-red flowers keeps flowering throughout the summer and its seeds can be collected and sown to produce an attractive border plant. The seeds provide food for a number of small birds around late summer. Due to its strong, erect stems the birds can alight and feed even in windy weather, when their feeding is an especial delight to watch.

A delightful flower that will add both beauty and scent to the bird garden is the meadowsweet (*Filipendula ulmaria*). To country folk it is known as 'Queen of the meadows', and its fragrant, foamy, creamy-white flowerheads line riverbanks, damp meadow, alder woods and pondside from early June until August. The seeds, which form in late August until October, are much sought after by some of the finches such as linnets and siskins. Once a plant is well established, its crown can be split and divided after cutting down the stems in October. The wild species, *F. ulmaria*, prefers a shady, moist situation, although the new species often favour sunny sites.

Seed collected from wild meadowsweet will provide plants up to 90 centimetres in height. It is a plant that likes a moist root run, so keep it well watered.

Oxford ragwort (*Senecio squalidus*), looking like a dwarf version of its common relative, apart from providing seeds for ground and low-feeding birds has a fascinating story to tell. It is not a truly British plant, its natural home being on the slopes of Mount Etna. Then, quite suddenly, in 1794, a few plants 'appeared' on walls around the Oxford Botanic Gardens and were seen by Linnaeus, the master craftsman of classification. How it got there is a mystery. Perhaps a traveller scraped his boots after visiting Sicily and so a few seeds settled on the wall beneath his window. Anyway, with the development and expansion of the railway, Oxford ragwort experienced a population explosion. Its wind-borne seeds, sucked along by passing trains, found the gravel embankment to be much like its native volcanic cinder soil and so it thrived. Where the railways went, the Oxford ragwort followed. Today it provides seeds for birds on railway embankments and rail yards everywhere, and now it is spreading along our motorways, its seeds drawn ever onward by speeding lorries. So today the birds benefit from a casual act of an unknown person two or three hundred years ago.

Table 2. Seed seasons.

| SEED PLANT | IN FLOWER | SEEDS AVAILABLE TO THE BIRDS | | | | | | | | | | | |
		Jan	Feb	Mar	April	May	June	July	Aug	Sept	Oct	Nov	Dec
Groundsel	all year	←---	---	---	---	---	---	---	---	---	---	---	---→
Oxford Ragwort	April					←---	---	---	---	---→			
Prickly Sowthistle	June							←---	---	---→			
Smooth Sowthistle	June							←---	---	---→			
Dandelion	April						←---	---→					
Wild Radish	May							←---	---	---→			
Charlock	May						←---	---→					
Spear Thistle	July							←---	---	---→			
Bristly Ox Tongue	June								←---	---→			
Knapweed	June									←---	---→		
Meadowsweet	June									←---	---→		
Burdock	July	←---	---	---→								←---	---→
Teasel	July	←---	---	---→									←---→
Chickweed	all year	←---	---	---	---	---	---	---	---	---	---	---	---→

The above table shows approximate flowering times and period of greatest seed numbers available. Locality and seasonal weather will affect these times, although they are all most sensitive to day length. Generally the flowering and subsequent seed-bearing dates of herbaceous plants are more regular than those of trees (see Table 1, p. 35).

When birds are feeding on the winter ground they invariably encounter the chickweed (*Stellaria media*), often described as one of the most persistent weeds of the garden and other cultivated land. It is regarded as a nuisance simply because its flowers produce seeds throughout the year with a peak from early summer to late autumn—and those seeds are just what the birds enjoy. It is an interesting plant which has a long line of hairs down the leaf stems and these collect mist drops and rain which are absorbed by the plant and help it to survive in difficult conditions. Collect from wild plants and grow the seeds on in a small container before transplanting. Although an annual, you should only need to plant once; after that it will self-seed.

There is another plant which also contributes its seed to the locked-up treasures in the soil, and is indeed a most prolific seed producer—the wild radish (*Raphanus raphanistrum*). A very common plant of both cultivated and waste places, its straggling growth habit will not endear it to you. However, it is a useful seed producer. One plant grows as many as 160 seed pods, each containing from four to seven seeds. Those that are not taken from the plant fall and provide food to be picked up from the ground later in the winter.

There are many more wild plants that can be introduced and with a little experience you may decide to try them. Do not be disappointed if your teasels are not visited by the birds or some other flourishing wild weed is apparently neglected. Bird visits to seeding plants are sometimes quite brief so you may have missed them. However, it is almost certain that a few of the birds visiting your bird table may have been encouraged there by the habitat you have created and they may well come again and again during ensuing weeks. There is so much to be learned about the ways in which we can attract birds to our garden that any day you may discover a simple clue that works wonders in your particular area.

WILD FLOWER GROUPINGS

Whilst there are many plants that will encourage birds purely for the seeds and berries they have to offer, every wild garden can be improved visually by including some of the wild flowering plants. Look along any hedgerow in spring or high summer and you will see how the hedge itself thrusts flowers galore from its tangled vegetation. To develop your wild area or garden, remember to plant out a few wild flowers under the trees. What better to start with than the lovely foxglove (*Digitalis purpurea*). Plant a group of about seven plants (they are easily grown from seed) under a spreading elder bush and the tall spikes of mauve flowers will blend beautifully with the white sprays of the elderberry. There are plenty of different colours to choose from when you buy foxglove seed but try to keep to the wild colour, it will blend in so much better. Interspersed with the tall spires sow a few common mallow (*Malva sylvestris*) which, although growing to some 90 cm in height, often sprawls over a small area, its large pinkish-purple flowers lasting for several weeks. A small group of red campion (*Silene dioicum*), sown so that they form a tight little clump, glow with rosy-pink and thrive in a close-knit community of flowers. And if you sow a small covering of red clover

Hogweed (Heracleum sphondylium) *and other umbellifers are architecturally beautiful plants for the bird garden. Their flowers attract insects and much of the plant may become home to large numbers of aphids, insects that blue tits find irresistible.*

Table 3. Wild flower flowering periods.

NAME OF FLOWER	Mar	April	May	June	July	Aug	Sept
Lesser Celandine	‹---------	-----------	---------›				
Red Campion		‹---------	-----------	-----------	---›	. . . . . .	. . . . . .
Herb Robert		‹---------	-----------	---------›	. . . . .	. . . . .	
Dovesfoot Cranesbill		‹---------	-----------	-----------	-----------	---›	. . . . . .
Dusky Cranesbill		‹---------	-----------	-----------	---------›	. . . . .	. . . . . .
Red Clover			‹---------	-----------	---›	. . . . .	. . .
Hogweed			‹---------	-----------	---------›		
Spindle Tree			‹---------	---------›			
Common Mallow				‹---------	-----------	---›	. . .
Hardhead (Knapweed)				‹---------	-----------	---------›	. . . . . .
Corn Poppy				‹---------	-----------	---›	. . . . . .
Cornflower				‹---------	-----------	---------›	
Meadow Cranesbill				‹---------	-----------	---›	. . .
Foxglove				‹---------	-----------	-----------	---------›
Wild Teasel					‹---------	---------›	
Spear Thistle					‹---------	-----------	---› . . .
Hemp Agrimony					‹---------	-----------	---------›
Marjoram					‹---------	-----------	---------›

These flowering periods will vary according to whether a garden is in the south or north, and flower formation is also affected by the weather conditions each year. Some flowers continue to flower almost every month of the year, as, for example, red campion in the south-west of England.

Seeds will begin to ripen according to species, from approximately four weeks after flowering commences, and some, like the spear thistle, continue to release seeds well after flowering ceases.

Opposite: Be bold in your use of wild flower groupings. Spend a while looking closely at the way they grow together in the wild. Then all you have to do is plant them that way in your garden and leave the rest to the birds. This grouping includes cocksfoot grass (Dactylis glomerata), *foxglove* (Digitalis purpurea), *common mallow* (Malva sylvestris) *and red campion* (Silene dioicum).

(*Trifolium pratense*) to clothe the soil you will have a rich red carpet to enjoy as well.

Another grouping might include some of the cranesbills such as meadow cranesbill (*Geranium pratense*) with its bright blue flowers with a hint of violet growing up to 60 cm tall and flowering from June onwards. Try dusky cranesbill (*Geranium phaeum*) which grows up to 60 cm in height with maroon flowers from mid May until early June. There are many different cranesbills so you will be able to choose from one of the wild flower producers' catalogues. Sow or plant out the seedlings under one of the tall umbellifers like hogweed (*Heracleum sphondylium*), a very architecturally-growing plant erect up to 120 cm. It is one of the commonest flowers of open sunny banks and will look best if three are grown together at the edge of a bramble thicket and under a honeysuckle-embraced rowan or whitebeam. You could even plant one or two among the wild radish or spear thistles.

A very attractive deciduous bush with intense red foliage and coral-pink berries in autumn is the spindle-tree (*Euonymus europaeus*). It will grow to a height of three or more metres on chalk or limestone where it forms thickets in the wild. But in crowded hedgerows it often forms small shrubs less than 90 cm in height, tending to spread rather than rise. It responds to winter clipping. Using this as a foreground against a hedge of escallonia Donard seedling, and with some wild teasel (*Dipsacus fullonum*) grouped to one side and a dog rose (*Rosa canina*) draping over the lower growing knapweed or hardhead (*Centaurea nigra*), you will have flowers combined with food for the birds.

There are innumerable permutations on the wild flower groupings you could enjoy, and quite the best way to get ideas is to go out to a stretch of wild country and take a really close look at the plant associations found in the green world. By so doing you will discover their relative flowering periods and then be able to take this into consideration when planting.

There is one little flower that must be included—the lesser celandine (*Ranunculus ficaria*). It will give you a bright and shining carpet just as winter departs and its lovely flowers herald warmer days to come.

SEED SOURCES

Wild flower seeds can be bought from the firms listed at the end of this book, and many nurseries and garden centres sell them along with the more usual garden species. If you store them in the garden shed you will probably find the envelopes nibbled and the seeds eaten by your friendly local mouse.

In nature wild flower seeds are dispersed a short period after flowering, but in my experience, since seeds remain viable for a very long time, they are best kept until the spring. However, sowing wild flower seed is not always the simple and successful business it is supposed to be. For instance, sowing by scattering the seed on a lawn or rough grass seldom results in any degree of success—there is simply too much competition from the established grass. By far the best way is to sow the seed in seedboxes or small plastic containers. Spread the seed sparingly and cover with a very thin sprinkling of compost. Keep away from frost. Finally,

Always remember to store your wild flower seeds and wild bird foods in a mouse-proof container. Long-tailed fieldmice take refuge from winter weather in garden sheds, leaving only empty husks after their nocturnal feasts.

when you have a selection of strong seedlings, you can plant them out in late March (maybe a little later in the north) into ready-prepared, friable soil. Plant them a little more closely than you intend the finished plants to be so that the thin and weakly ones can be eliminated later on.

Despite the vigorous and abundant growth you may have seen in meadows, wild flowers are not always easy to grow in the garden, but with care you will be successful. Like all young, living things, they need that extra attention in their first few weeks of life.

CEREALS

Whilst cereals are not regarded as 'wild' plants, they fulfil a function when sown in your garden among the wild flowers. Cereals are high priority on many birds' visiting lists. The best way to introduce them to your garden is to clear a patch measuring about a square metre and in that area to sow a single species such as wheat or oats. Sow the seed thickly, about 2 cm deep, and having done so cover with whatever 'bird preventing' device you favour—a few pieces of paper strung from a stick, or better still cover them with a piece of small mesh wire netting raised a few inches above the soil—for alas, birds will find that seed if you fail to protect it.

Not only are cereals attractive when grown in clumps, but at harvest time their golden colour is a pleasant addition to any bird garden. And best of all the birds will enjoy the seeds.

No peat, please!

As a wildlife lover you can help to save our disappearing peatlands, now that a genuine alternative is available. Wessex Horticultural Products are producing Cocopeat, a renewable resource made from coconut husks. It has a spongelike consistency capable of holding large quantities of water, and with a pH of 5 is a fine garden ingredient for composts. It is a by-product of the coir-fibre industry and has been used in Sri Lanka for many years. It is ready sterilised and therefore weed-free. Altogether an excellent alternative to peat for making up seed or potting composts and for starting off all your bird garden plants. However, many firms are experimenting with peat replacement products, so keep an eye on the horticultural press and look for some of them at your local garden centre.

4
FOOD, FEEDING PLACES AND DRINKING SITES

The siting of a bird table and drinking place is inevitably a conflict between having it in a safe, non-predator situation, yet at the same time keeping it within observation distance of the house.

Birds like to approach a table from a safe perch nearby, and a cat-proof tree or tall bush within a few metres is ideal. A table placed on a pole at least two metres high from the ground is sufficiently safe, but its actual dimensions are a matter of personal choice. However, it seems logical to me that a tiny table is less attractive than a large one, simply because birds like feeding space between each other. Provide holes in the base and spaces in the surrounding 'wall' to permit free drainage of rain, and a sloping roof will help keep the food dry.

If the table is a large one, nail one or two wooden battens from side to side so as to prevent the food blowing up into one end. You can even use these compartments for different foods so that the different species of birds are able to feed apart.

Try and arrange to erect your bird table in the late summer so that birds may become used to it, and then by the time the first inclement weather arrives you will be all set for feeding.

Winter is the time supreme for feeding birds in the garden, for that is the time of year when they often live from day to day. All night long in the cold winter winds, feathers fluffed to preserve warmth, the birds consume the stored energy laid down as fat from the previous day's feeding. A hungry bird going to roost when the frost bites deeply will be lucky to survive unless it can consume plenty of rich food the following day. It has been found that, of the fat laid down during the day, about half is used up during the night.

During intense cold and wet spells many birds feed eagerly, in the early morning and late at night, so as a bird gardener you should remember to put the food out as early as possible and to provide another supply an hour before dusk. In those few exceptionally cold winter spells when the blizzards stream out from Siberia, birds will continue to feed throughout the day. It is then that even the blackbirds find difficulty in turning over the hard-frozen dead leaves or penetrating snow cover to find the few little forms of life that help them to satisfy hunger on more pleasant days.

Winter food for the table can be provided from household scraps. Bacon rind, cheese rind (seldom seen today), bread, cake and chopped apples are all available without raiding the fridge or pantry. But for the really energy-giving foods try one of the proprietary packed seeds. One of the best, in my own experience, is produced by C.J. Wildbird Foods Ltd., The Rea, Upton Magna, Shrewsbury SY4 4UB. Their variety and quality are quite excellent and the packaging is tidy, neat

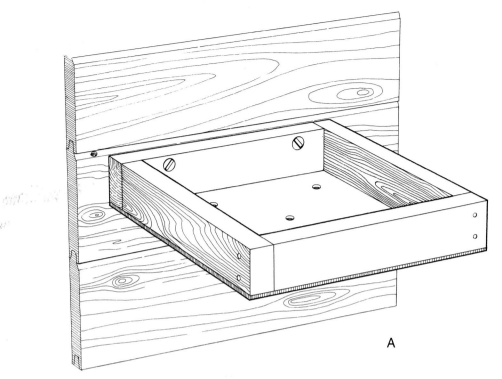

A ready-made small bird table can be fixed to a garden shed or wall (A), or attached to a window frame or window-sill (B). One of the better made seed boxes can also be used.

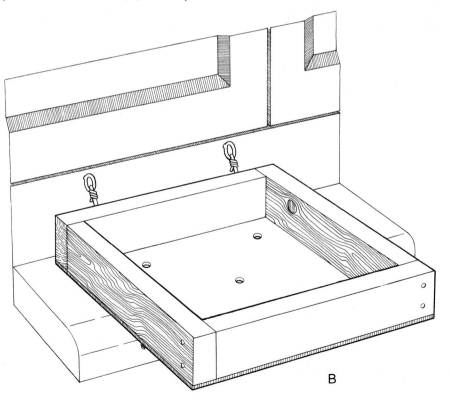

Interesting feeding tests can be devised by providing compartments on your bird table and filling them with different foods. By careful observation of feeding birds you may discover a little more about each species' preferences. Remember to make some drainage holes to prevent waterlogging.

and easy of access. At the time of writing they are offering a new 'peckerpak' as a starter selection which contains 4 kg peanuts, 4 kg peanut granules, 5 kg greenfinch brand birdseed and 6 siskin brand red bags for peanuts. The pack is delivered free by Securicor fourteen days from receipt of order (mainland UK only). Their birdseed mixture contains wheat as a bulk, canary seed, red and yellow millet, kibbled maize, flaked or micronised maize, pinhead oatmeal, peanut granules, sunflower seeds of three kinds of which the black is excellent, and a small quantity of hemp. If you prefer to order the greenfinch birdseed, sunflower seed, dakota red millet, canary seed, peanuts (aflatoxin free), peanut granules or siskin brand red bags separately, they can be obtained in 50 kg, 25 kg or 12½ kg packs.

Another firm supplying foods is Ernest Charles & Co. Ltd., Heathpark, Honiton, Devon EX14 8SE. They do a Wild Bird Special Menu in 6 kg, 12.5 kg, 25 kg, and 50 kg packs of mixed seeds including sunflower, wheat, flaked maize, peanuts and a whole range of small seeds. Peanut kernels and peanuts in shell are available in similar packs.

John E. Haith, Park Street, Cleethorpes, South Humberside DN35 7NF, supply wild bird food and sunflower seeds (small, striped and mixed) in packs of 3½ lbs., 7 lbs., 14 lbs., 21 lbs., 28 lbs., 56 lbs. and 112 lbs.

MAKING A PIE FOR THE BIRDS

First you need some sort of container—a small polythene or plastic pudding basin, or half an empty coconut shell will do nicely. I have often used small plastic pots, too. Drill or pierce a small hole near the rim; later, when the container is filled, you can attach a piece of wire to suspend it from a branch. Incidentally, if you are not too fussy about appearance, a plastic margarine container is quite useful.

Now for the ingredients. Experience with a variety of fillings has tended to show that the most popular with the birds are a sprinkling of currants and sultanas, ditto of corn and chopped pieces of bacon rind, a few chopped pieces of apple and a liberal quantity of mixed bird seed and peanuts. Quantities are difficult to assess, but the ingredients should at least equal the amount of suet. If you prefer to make your bird pies with a prepared mixture, John E. Haith (address given above) supplies an excellent Birdcake Mixture comprising biscuit rusk, wheatmeal, peanuts, sunflower seeds and other bird seeds. Simply mix two parts of the mixture with one part fat or dripping.

Next, a visit to the butcher to buy a couple of pounds of suet. Back home cut it into plum-sized pieces and place on a *very* low heat, preferably in a non-stick pan. Let it simmer until much of the suet has melted into a golden liquid fat. This process is a bit smelly so keep the kitchen window open.

Having mixed the ingredients together and balanced the container at an angle, put a small quantity into it and then add a little melted suet. Repeat this process until the container is full. Leave it to set firm and cool down. Having pushed a knobbly twig into it so that it extends 10 cm beyond the rim, all you have to do is hang it up and wait for the birds to come—usually starlings, tits and a very occasional chaffinch. It will take four or five days before it is regularly visited— after that you will be forever making bird pies.

Bird pies like these, apart from being suspended below the bird table, can be hung in mature trees. Whilst it is more interesting to watch the concentrated activity at the table, a few isolated pies spread around the garden are highly attractive to birds. And since plastic containers look a little unsightly, you may prefer to use a small earthenware bowl. When filling the former, push a cork into the drainage hole or plug firmly with a wad of paper. Either can be removed when the suet has set firm.

Pies for the bird table
The same preparation process can be used to make a pie for birds on the bird table. You simply use a margarine container and when the pie has cooled off and the suet gone hard, partially immerse the container in a bowl of hot water. This loosens the pie and it can be tipped upside down onto the table.

These pies can contain tiny pieces of crust, cake crumbs, bird seed and peanuts, and once the birds are used to the appearance of the mould it is surprising what a wide variety will feed on it.

WARNING! Birds at work
Always remember to stop offering pies, and indeed fat and peanuts in any form,

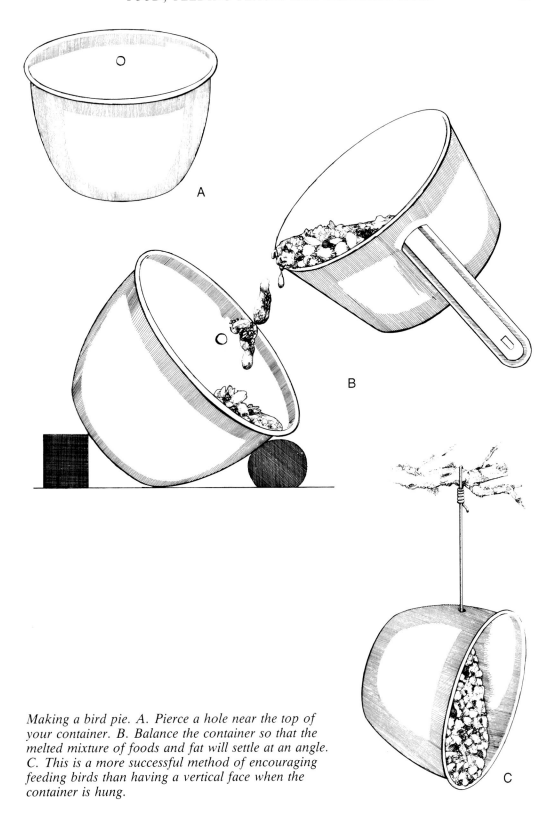

Making a bird pie. A. Pierce a hole near the top of your container. B. Balance the container so that the melted mixture of foods and fat will settle at an angle. C. This is a more successful method of encouraging feeding birds than having a vertical face when the container is hung.

well before the nesting season starts, usually at the beginning of March. Baby birds cannot digest quantities of fat and they need natural foods which would normally be found in the wild environment.

REARING MEALWORMS FOR ROBINS

Mealworms are the larval stage of the small beetle *Tenebrio molitor* which breeds in bran and is an ideal insect larva to feed to robins. Rearing them in quantity is not difficult. You need a metal biscuit or cake tin forming about a 25–30 cm cube. Perforate most of the lid with small holes—a hammer and a 5 cm nail perform perfectly—to let air in.

Now drop in a mixture of wholemeal flour and porridge oats (equal parts) to a depth of about 15 cm. On top put a 7 cm layer of bran. Push 2 cm thick slices of potato well into the mixture and lay a piece of thick damp cloth over the surface (a piece of flannel trousers, old blanket or hessian is ideal).

The starter pack for mealworms will entail a visit to the local pet shop, where you should buy a few ounces of mealworms. Spread them under the cloth and

Mealworm container. A. Small holes in lid for ventilation. B. A few layers of damp cloth over the top of the food. C. Bran. D. Wholemeal flour and porridge oats. E. Pieces of potato, carrot or turnip. After a few days the layers intermix and the cloth will require to be redampened.

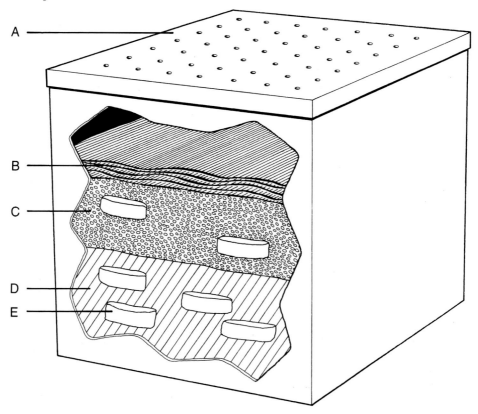

leave the tin in as warm a room as possible. A cold room slows the entire process down, while a widely variable temperature is not to be recommended, and placing it on the central heating boiler or radiator will simply 'cook' them. An ideal constant temperature is around 21°C.

Every fourth or fifth day, slice a potato or carrot and place a couple of slices or more into the mixture, removing the old ones as you do so. This will help provide the moisture needed. Remember also to re-dampen the cloth whenever it dries out.

Periodically, and the time will vary according to the number of insects feeding, the food supply will degenerate into a dusty deposit and should be replaced by a fresh supply of meal.

Once the breeding tin is established you will see mealworms (larvae), pupae, and adult beetles milling around. Freshly emerged beetles are creamy-white with tan-coloured heads and adult beetles dark brown. The eggs laid on the food will be too small to see with the naked eye.

If breeding seems a little more effort than you are willing to exert you can simply buy 25 or 50 g from the pet shop and keep them in a tin. They will survive well as long as you offer a small quantity of food. Twenty-five grams of mealworms should last you—if you put out a dozen to eighteen a day—ten days or more.

Encouraging your local robin to come for them needs a little patience and careful observation. If you watch your robin you will soon discover it shows a preference for a certain part of the garden and often perches or flits about in a particular bush. That's the place to put the mealworm feeder.

Robin's snackbar

The feeder needs to be about 50–75 mm square or in diameter and some 65 mm deep. It can be plastic, wood or metal. Drill a few very small holes in the base, making sure they are too small for the mealworms to escape through, and then drill four more holes, one near the centre of the rim on each side. Attach wire and form a hook about 30 cm up to suspend it.

Hang it in the situation where you know the robin spends some time, preferably among some foliage and not exposed in an open situation. Alternatively you can fix the feeder to the corner of your bird table. Put about eight mealworms in the feeder *and be patient*. It may be several days before the robin decides it is safe to eat there. In the waiting period, especially if the weather is cool, you may find one or two of the mealworms have formed pupae. No problem: robins enjoy pupae too. However, when you are trying to introduce your robin to the snackbar it is best to keep the feeder stocked with fresh and lively mealworms.

In my experience, our robins have always seemed to prefer visiting to feed around mid-morning and early evening. You should replenish the food supply as soon as the previous batch has been eaten.

Feeding robins in this way is a most satisfying experience, chiefly because you will feel you have a very close association with a small bird. Remember, however, that the very best time of year to offer the mealworms is from September through the winter and even longer if the robin keeps coming.

Robin's snackbar. A small wooden or plastic container should be screwed to the side of your bird table. A dozen or so mealworms, early morning and evening, are 'just what the robin ordered'. In some gardens the container attracts more quickly if hung among bushes where the robin is known to spend a little time. Blue tits often take more than their share.

A FEW FACTS ABOUT PEANUTS

The 'safe nuts' scheme was initiated by the Birdfood Standards Association to encourage dealers to sell only those peanuts free from aflatoxin, a toxin produced by a fungus which grows when the nuts are stored in humid conditions or have not been dried properly when gathered.

During warm, damp spells of weather, the last few nuts left in a feeder quickly develop fungus growths. To prevent this happening thoroughly wash and clean the container as soon as only a few nuts are left. Unless you do this, and continue to top up the container—especially if it has a plastic or wood base—a few nuts on the baseplate will inevitably develop fungus, so it is much better partly to fill the container which will result in a quicker transfer of nuts from holder to birds. Incidentally, chaffinches, dunnocks, collared doves and robins prefer to take their nuts spread on the bird table. With more than 10,000 tons of peanuts sold for wild bird feeding each year, they must surely form a substantial part of the diet of many garden birds.

One of the problems associated with putting out food is the never-ending appetite of starlings. Once they descend on your table they will clear the entire table of food. An effective yet unsightly method of control is to drape a length of wire netting around the table, and as long as you keep to a hole diameter of about 30 mm, the starlings will be thwarted. To my mind, however, they are as entitled to food as any other garden bird and I partially discourage them by putting out a limited quantity of bread about ten o'clock every morning. The hungry flock, waiting in a nearby tree, descend and gobble it up and then go off to other feeding places in the neighbourhood. In the meantime, I put out food for the other quieter birds. This usually works well, but just occasionally those starlings surprise me by either hanging around or arriving unexpectedly off schedule. But surely that is all part of the pleasure of birds, for they are often unpredictable and there is always so much to learn simply by watching them. And one thing is certain, they always respond to our care and attention.

Table 4. Spot their favourite foods.

SPECIES	Berries	Cereals	Fruit	Insects	Molluscs	Scraps	Seeds	Spiders	Worms
Blackbird	o		o		o	o	o	o	o
Blue Tit		o	o	o			o	o	
Chaffinch		o	o	o			o	o	
Coal Tit				o			o	o	
Collared Dove	o	o	o			o	o		
Dunnock				o			o		
Great Tit			o	o	o	o	o	o	o
Greenfinch	o	o		o			o		
House Sparrow		o		o		o	o		o
Robin	o		o	o			o	o	o
Starling			o	o	o	o		o	o
Wren				o			o	o	

SMALL BIRD TABLES FOR SMALL GARDENS

A table about 30 sq cm in area is better than none and if you have a place from which to suspend it, it can be made as shown. Light chain can be bought at your local DIY shop, or if you prefer you can suspend it on wire. The actual table should be made of 25 mm thick timber with 50 mm high walls. The extra weight will help to keep it steady in strong winds which have a tendency to scatter the food. As with all bird tables, provide holes or thin spaces to permit rain to drain away. Suspended bird tables have the added advantage that they can be placed to be safe from surprise attacks by the local cat.

A small table like this can be used in conjunction with a nut dispenser suspended below it and in that way the nut feeders, like greenfinch and tits, are able to feed whilst the others fill up on the table above. If you want to keep starlings away, you can use wire netting as suggested on p. 68.

Another idea for a small garden is to fix a small table below an opening window and resting on the sill. A slight problem with this situation is that if there is undue movement or possible occasional noise, as in a kitchen, the birds will be exceedingly shy and infrequent in their visits.

FOOD DISPENSERS

There is an ever increasing abundance of seed dispensers appearing in shops. They vary in size and efficiency and all too often it is difficult to gauge how attractive (or repellent!) they may be to the birds. Some that I have tried were absolutely useless. There are two factors to be aware of. The first is the tendency of some designs that incorporate a seed hopper to jam whenever a few large seeds, like sunflower, slide down together. Secondly, some suspended designs are so light that they swing about in the wind and scatter the seed far and wide. Of course the birds are still able to feed on the ground, but it is an invitation to lurking predators, and anyway the original purpose of the hopper was to provide food as required and at a safe height.

Because we seem to live in a plastic age, by far the greatest majority of seed hoppers are made of this substance. Many incorporate a plastic tube to hold the seed, with a dispenser device at the bottom, and whilst they work efficiently, you cannot see how much seed is left without opening it up. Those that incorporate a glass container may be more expensive but at least you know how the seed situation is.

As a general rule, choose a feeder that has ample space—one which will hold a pint glassful of seed, otherwise you will be forever refilling it.

Peanut dispensers
The red plastic-netted bags, sometimes referred to as siskin bags, are quite popular. They have a plastic fastener device which enables easy refilling and are certainly popular with the tit family, greenfinches, sparrow and starlings. They need to be examined regularly as the netting tears and not only releases the nuts, but can entangle birds' feet.

A second type consists of a plastic or wooden base surmounted by a steel mesh cylinder with a removable plastic top that has a ring for suspension. This sort and the previous one are the most common. Both are easy to keep clean, which is a highly important advantage especially in nut dispensers, as the last few nuts tend to consolidate and decay on the base unless frequently brushed clean.

In a recent observation test in our garden, a red plastic siskin bag and two square mesh tubular dispensers, one 45 cm long and the other 20 cm long, were hung on the bird table. The dispensers were fully filled with peanuts and observed for four days. In that time (early November) blue tits, coal tits, greenfinches and sparrows came to feed. The recorded percentages of the total number feeding were as follows:

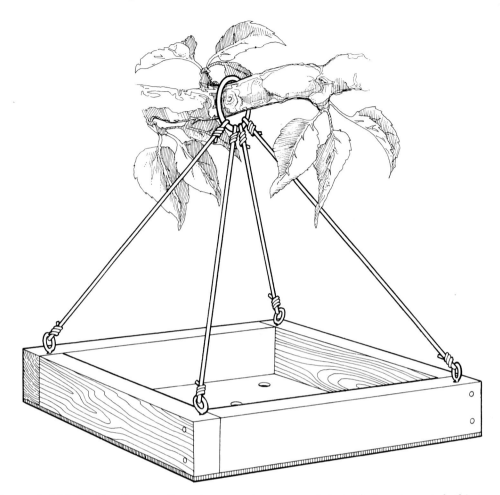

Suspended bird table. For small gardens or where an upright table is not wanted, this type can be suspended from the branch of a tree. If possible select a sheltered situation and check thoroughly for cat access before fixing in place.

Long tubular dispenser	60 per cent
Short tubular dispenser	34 per cent
Red plastic siskin bag	6 per cent

Should you prefer to buy your peanuts in their pale cream husks, and furthermore should you enjoy spending a little time in preparing your bird food, then the following method is recommended. Take a 38 cm length of galvanised wire and twist one end into a small circle. Holding a nut against a piece of wood, push the other end of the wire through the centre of the husk and push the nut down to the end. Repeat until the wire is nearly filled, then bend the top end into a sealed hook. The one disadvantage with this kind of feeder is that it is quickly emptied and so has to be regularly re-strung. But surely that's what we want, for the quicker it is empty, the better the birds have fed and we are really getting a response from our bird visitors.

THE GREY SQUIRREL

Whilst many wildlife enthusiasts would be delighted to have a visiting squirrel in their garden, bird lovers are often more guarded in their pleasure. The first problem presented by the arrival of a squirrel is the damage done to peanut dispensers. Their agility enables them to seize such containers placed in positions one would consider to be squirrel-proof, and their appetite is enormous. Once having found a free and easy supply of peanuts they will be regular visitors.

Try hanging your nut dispenser on the end of a piece of *very thin* wire at least a metre in length, the other end being secured to a branch.

Jamie Wood Ltd. Birds, Cross Street, Polegate, East Sussex BN26 6BN (Tel: 03212 3813) advertises in *Birds* magazine a bird table stated to be squirrel- and starling-proof on its upper deck. It might be worth trying one of these if you are pestered by squirrels.

The same firm offers a 'giant heavy-duty all metal feeder that really stops squirrels'.

Another way in which a bird table on the lawn can be protected is by a large metal funnel attached to the pole—as long as the squirrel cannot leap from a tree onto the bird table roof!

But whatever you do, the little animal will prove a problem and it will most certainly reach down and grasp those red siskin peanut bags and rip them to pieces to liberate the peanuts.

If you discover a 100 per cent anti-squirrel device, please let me know, or better still, let *Birds* magazine know the idea. It will be more than welcome.

If you are determined to exclude starlings there is a special tit feeder marketed by Eagle Products, 1 Eagle Close, Felixstowe, Suffolk IP11 7SE, which—and I quote—'feeds nuts to Blue tits, Great tits, Coal tits and Nuthatches ONLY and NOT to Starlings, Greenfinches and Sparrows.'

BATHING AND DRINKING PLACES

Very small bathing and drinking places can be made by adapting old sinks, plastic or pottery dishes and so on, but these still need places on which the birds can stand not more than knee deep. As with every small pond that has been built purely for the birds, it will need regular (say twice-yearly) cleaning. Birds like pure, clear water just the same as we do and it is surprising how quickly a small pond can become polluted.

Perhaps because, in an ordinary garden, we seldom see birds drinking, there is a tendency for us to overlook the importance of water. Most garden centres hold a range of bird bath/drinking devices most of which are raised on pillars. The actual water container is made from a variety of materials such as plastic, cement, waterproofed earthenware or china, but when you buy one try to choose it for its

Opposite: This type of feeder is claimed to be squirrel-proof, being all metal and heavy duty with a double layer of protective galvanised mesh holding 1½lbs of peanuts. Obtainable from Jamie Wood.

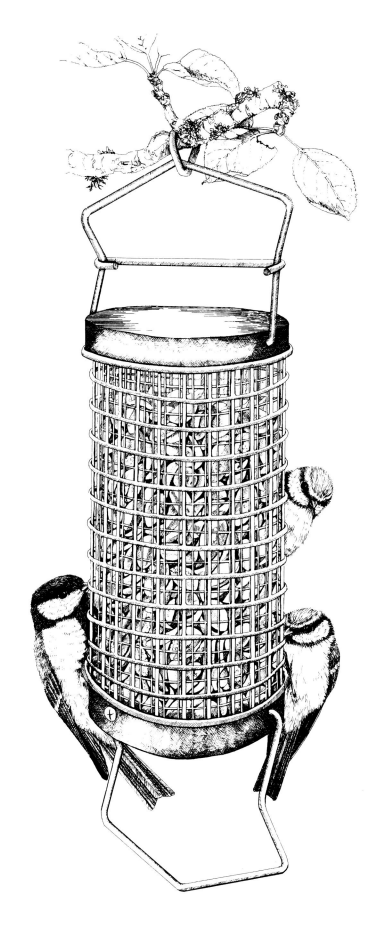

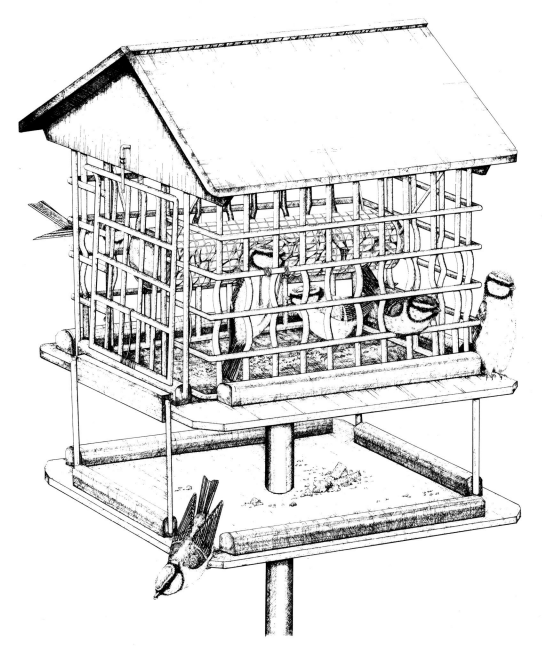

Since squirrels can be so destructive of so many feeders, this Jamie Wood 'Sussex' table has been designed for goldcrests, blue, willow, coal and great tits. It is starling- and squirrel-proof, allowing access to small birds only. The lower deck caters for all-comers, especially thrushes, blackbirds, finches and robins. It has an aluminium pole for soft ground or a special base for patios.

usefulness to the birds rather than its decorative appeal. Baths and drinking areas do need to be practical and it is vital to provide somewhere for the birds to alight and drink.

In especially cold winter conditions natural water supplies become locked up under ice; in hot summers, water evaporates very quickly; in both instances you will need to keep a close eye on water levels. I know it is sometimes recommended that you add substances to prevent freezing, but I would advise against this. Pure water is essential at all times and all seasons.

Birds dehydrate quite quickly so a frequent drink is essential to the well-being of many species. And in intense cold conditions water freezes very rapidly even after the ice is broken and removed. The best answer is to put an aquarium heater with a thermostat under some sand in the base of the drinking device. A very low wattage heater is all you need, but have it installed by a qualified electrician, since water and electricity can be deadly both to yourself and to the birds. Such heater/thermostats can be purchased at any good pet shop and since the amount of energy

A. Many types of water containers can be used as garden drinking baths for birds. Whilst they should be firmly fixed, they will also have to be easily removed for frequent cleaning. Heavy containers are better than light ones. B. A simple but effective drinking place can be assembled on a pole. If the container is light it should be held in place by a retaining border, but a heavy container is preferable.

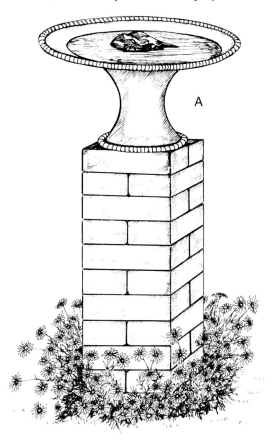

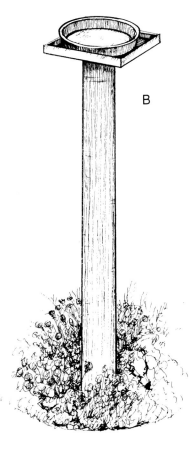

consumed is minimal and you will only switch it on when very cold weather threatens, the running costs are very small.

Another method, but more time-consuming, is to keep breaking the ice when it forms, scoop it out and replace with warm water. But in really cold conditions it will freeze up again in less than two hours.

Water *depth* is an important factor and if you have a sizeable bird bath/drinking vessel place one or two suitably sized stones that just break the water surface — or better still slope down into the water—so that the birds can drink without having to bend nearly double.

In the limited space of a small garden there may only be room to provide water on the bird table. In that event the container used should be of heavy material and with no overhanging edges on which birds can alight and tip it up—frightening themselves as well as going without a drink. Plastic dishes, often with outward leaning sides, are quite unsuitable; tins or light metal containers have edges which are too sharp for perching; tall dishes are easily blown or tipped over. So use a squat, heavy dish with a good wide rim to alight on, and before deciding to use it give it a thorough 'tip-up' test. Not all birds drink regularly, so do not worry if you seldom see one drinking; if you have provided the facility you have helped in the most practical way possible.

Since birds have to keep their plumage in good condition, preening and bathing are essential aspects of their behaviour, and quite the best place to bathe—and also to drink—is the garden bird pond. But a number of factors should be considered at the planning stage.

Siting the pond
Siting a pond is most important both for its beauty and its utility. Ideally it should be in partial shade, or at least protected from the midday sun, for this not only

Any drinking vessel on a bird table should be heavily built, small and placed in one corner. It will require daily cleaning, sometimes twice a day when winds blow seed husks and pieces of food into it. Clean water is essential.

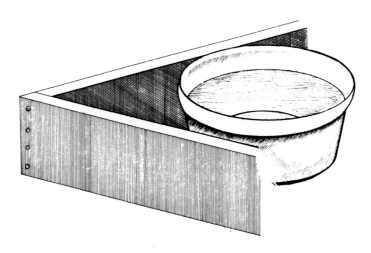

prevents the water heating up but cuts down the excessive light that inevitably turns clarity into green pea soup. Green algae are the bane of garden ponds and they grow for two main reasons. Firstly, they thrive on any accumulating minerals in the water caused by the decay of last year's fallen leaves; and secondly, in the presence of sunlight, they suddenly undergo a population explosion. Occasionally a third factor comes into play, and that is the absence of competitors. A pond rich in plant growth seldom turns green, simply because the plants are feeding on—and therefore removing—those minerals so that the algae do not stand a chance. Shade can be provided by a tree, preferably an evergreen, but if you decide to use a deciduous one you will have to provide some sort of cover during the brief period of leaf fall—netting of some kind usually suffices. Remember that the leaves of surrounding trees may also blow into the pond! But this is only a temporary problem and most of the year should prove to be incident-free.

A pond for the birds
Most pet shops, garden centres and nurseries now sell a great variety of ready-made ponds. They are usually plastic or fibreglass, and whilst they are very attractive for the growing of water lilies and keeping a few goldfish, few of them are designed to cater for birds. One problem is that they are too deep. Admittedly you can place a large stone in the water so that its surface is just under the water level, but inevitably that level drops in hot weather and rises in rain storms, so you are constantly adjusting it by adding water when needed.

When choosing a plastic pond select one that has plenty of shallow water areas for the establishment of boggy places, for these are essential if you want to encourage birds.

Having made your purchase you will need to outline the pond shape in the soil and dig it out. Go about 50 mm deeper than the pond so that the base of your excavation can be filled with sand to form a firm base for the plastic to rest upon. After you have inserted the pond, cover its edges with turf which can overlap by as much as 25 mm. It will soon become part of the pond, and even overhang the water surface for a few centimetres. This eliminates the unsightly plastic edge and a few large, flat stones can be added at this stage.

Building your own pond
Construction of a pond using a plastic sheet is another method and this has a slight advantage over the prefabricated kind because it enables you to create your own design. All garden centres and many large DIY stores sell pond liners and you can choose between butyl or pvc. Butyl is strong and is usually supplied off a roll in a black colour, although more expensive forms have a coloured material welded on to the butyl. Given average careful treatment it is tough, weather-resistant and free from any tendency to decay. When working out how much you need, you must remember to allow plenty of material for the depth and also estimate for an overlap of at least 30 centimetres outwards from the pool's edge.

One essential in planning your pond is to ensure that it is *level*. I know, it sounds obvious! But it is surprising how easy it is, having established levels, to

A decorative surround and a few flowers add to the liveliness of the drinking place. Use dual-purpose flowers like asters which provide colour in summer and seeds for the birds in the autumn. Always do all you can to make it safe from cats. Aster amellus 'King George' and A. novi belgii 'Patricia Ballard' (pink).

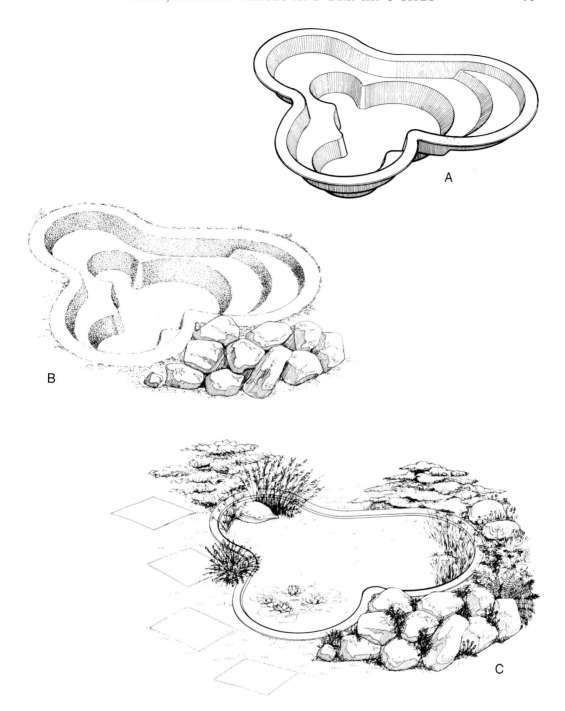

A. Fibreglass ponds come ready made. B. By careful planning and marking out of the ground remove soil to the same contours as those of the pond. The removed soil can be arranged to form a mound which, with the addition of a few stones, becomes a rockery. C. The rim of the pond can be left visible, but is better covered if the finished effect is to be informal. Emergent plants and a strategically placed rock provide a place for birds to both drink and bathe.

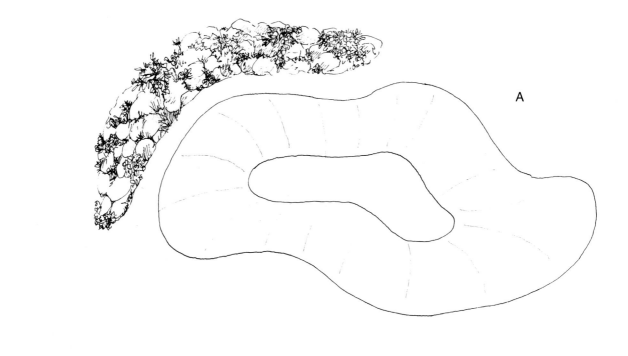

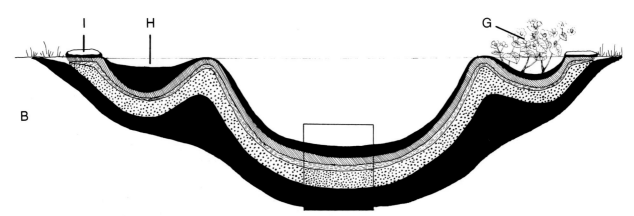

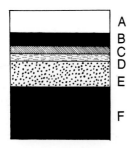

A. Excavate the hollow to whatever shape you fancy, using the removed soil to make a bank or rockery or even a raised surround.

B. Cross-section of butyl-lined pond to show detail: (a) water area; (b) soil and mud; (c) butyl or similar waterproof plastic; (d) protective layer to prevent damage to plastic. Material such as felt, old blankets, plastic sacks can be used; (e) layer of fine sand as cushion for plastic; (f) soil; (g) marginal plants; (h) shallow area for marsh and bog plants; (i) rockwork around edge to hold butyl down.

forget them during construction and to end up with a pond which has one end wall three inches above the water level.

At this stage, decide where to place the overflow. This is normally a pipe leading the water well away from the pond. Whatever your pond material you should incorporate some kind of overflow system, although allowing the water to overflow over the rim causes very few problems and, from the birds' point of view, is an advantage. They are able to reach the water very easily.

When outlining your pond on the soil remember that you will need sloping sides—an angle of 35 to 45 degrees will be ideal. Such a slope not only makes the pond more natural but facilitates the laying of concrete along the sides.

The third method is to build in brick or cement blocks and concrete. It may sound formidable but in fact is quite simple if you follow a few basic rules. First, dig out the soil to the shape you have marked out and, since your pond should be about 45 centimetres deep, clear away the soil to a depth of 60 centimetres. This will allow for the addition of 7.5 centimetres of rubble (stones and broken brick) which should be well beaten down into the base so that the surface of the finished rubble layer is now about 52.5 centimetres deep.

Next, prepare your concrete mix. Ordinary cement is fine but you should incorporate a prescribed amount of waterproofer which most builders' merchants supply. A mix of one part cement to two parts sharp sand and three parts aggregate (fine or crushed gravel) should be very thoroughly mixed with the waterproofing agent. This is the hard part of the operation, but small cement mixers can be hired quite cheaply from tool hire firms and they certainly make light work of the job. Add this concrete mix to the rubble base and stamp it down well so that it incorporates, then finish off by levelling it. If the pond base is more than two square metres it is best to incorporate some steel mesh reinforcement in the middle of this concrete layer.

The pond walls can be made either with concrete or built up with bricks or cement blocks. Either way you will have provided a sloping earth side to your original excavation, and this should include some ledges and shallow areas for plants. When the concrete base is semi-dry, using an old screwdriver or similar sharp implement, scratch a criss-cross pattern for at least 15 centimetres all round the outer edge of the base. This provides roughness for the cement or concrete to key into.

Now let the base concrete dry.

Next, if you are using concrete walls, carefuly apply a 5–7.5 cm layer of concrete to the sloping walls. This should be done in one operation all the way round, thus avoiding joins that inevitably result in future cracks and seepage. Carefully shape the concrete into the ledges and hollows and leave the surface fairly smooth.

You are now ready for the next stage. As the wall begins to set, mix one part cement with three parts sand plus the waterproofing agent and a colourant powder if you so desire. These colours are usually red or green, and whilst the red matches well in a sandstone area, the green is more pondlike, although after a few months ordinary cement will in any case turn green as the microscopic plants coat it. Spread this mix over the concrete wall and overlap the base for at least a foot.

Smooth and leave to dry. If it is a hot, sunny day, plenty of wet newspapers should be laid over the concrete or cement to prevent too-rapid drying. And keep it dampened until sunset.

One last word of advice regarding the use of cement and concrete: always add a quantity of waterproofing agent, even when bricklaying.

It sounds like a great deal of hard work, but the reward is a pond that will last for years and look very attractive.

Newly made cement ponds need about a month to mature and to rid the water of any contaminates that may leach out of the concrete. Change the water several times to hasten the process.

The next task is to fill in the various hollows, ledges and very shallow places with a suitable soil mixture. Incorporate at least fifty per cent by bulk of humus, either from a compost heap or whatever source you choose. These days we should try to avoid the use of peat purely on conservation grounds and the protection of the few remaining peatlands of our country. Most of these areas are extremely important bird places either as habitats or migratory feeding and resting or over-wintering places, where birds can enjoy a little peace away from human disturbance.

So at last you are ready for the exciting part—choosing and planting out the flowers and foliage that will create the ideal bird bathing and drinking area.

PLANTS FOR THE BIRD POND

A well planted pond is not only attractive to the eye but is most certainly a very big attraction to the birds who, once they know it is there, will constantly visit. In most town environments open shallow water is a scarce commodity and even in rural countryside, more and more ponds and ditches are being drained. Hence water is at a premium.

Once again we can look to the wild green environment with its natural ponds. Nearly all have shallow sloping banks with plenty of puddly pools left by the feet of drinking cattle. Here grow the marginal plants such as meadowsweet (*Filipendula ulmaria*) which will thrive in marshy soil and later produce seeds which finches enjoy. But its main function is to provide a little height where birds may alight. Another magnificent and tall marshy plant is the great willowherb or codlins-and-cream (*Epilobium hirsutum*). It displays itself best next to meadowsweet because of its contrasting rose-coloured flowers. For late summer flowering include one or two purple loosestrife (*Lythrum salicaria*) with its tapering bright purple flowers. Try to find room, too, for the yellow iris or flag (*Iris pseudacorus*): its leaves alone make a striking feature against the water surface and the rich yellow flowers add

Opposite: *Concrete or brick-lined pond.*
A. Soil removed to required shape. Overflow fitted. Whilst vertical walls are easier to construct, you may prefer to slope them at about 45°. B. Rubble base. C. Side walls can be built of brick, concrete blocks or poured concrete behind shuttering. D. A layer of waterproofed cement is plastered over entire inside surface. E. Plant out and be patient whilst the plants begin to grow.

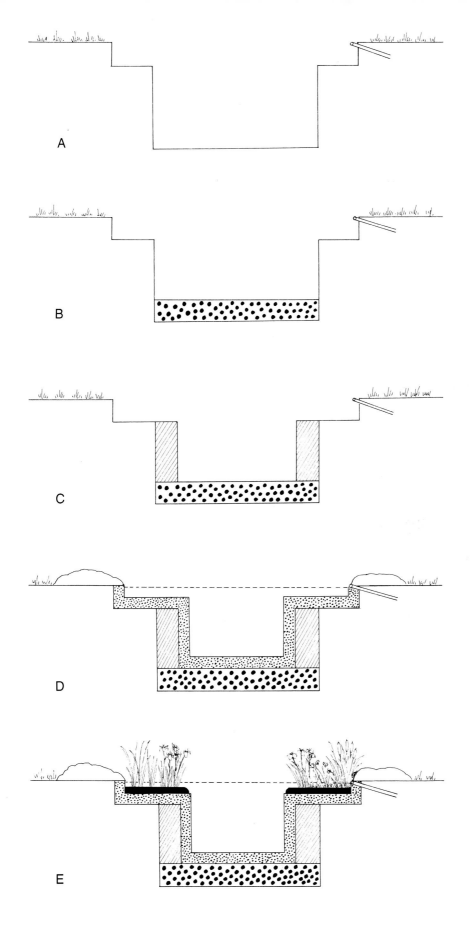

A

B

C

D

E

to the general appeal of the plant. It is one of the commonest of the wild iris, and since a bird garden should resemble as nearly as possible its wild counterpart, plant this species in preference to some of the more flamboyant cultivated varieties. It likes its roots in water and will thrive as long as it does not dry out. It is a hardy perennial, typical of the pondside.

In complete contrast are the delicate flowers of the water forget-me-not (*Myosotis scorpioides*), a beautiful creeping perennial with massed cobalt blue, 7 mm flowers that delight the eye from June into July with a few remaining on into August. Plant it in wet soil where its roots will be constantly submerged and it will reward you with a show of flowers, low down among the rich green growth of its oval leaves.

Three plants which in my opinion are essential to the establishment of a natural pond are the reed (*Phragmites communis*) and the bulrush or great reedmace (*Typha latifolia*) and also the lesser reedmace (*Typha angustifolia*). All three add stature to the surrounds as well as providing that sense of wildness that seems to attract birds. The reed (*P. communis*) quickly establishes itself and providing it is left unchecked will colonise a corner of the pond. By careful control it can be persuaded to extend along the pond's edge and in a matter of some three years will provide a pleasant screen in which its wispy flowerheads sigh in the breeze, while in winter the crisp rattle of its dried leaves brush lightly against the bamboo-like stems.

I am convinced that features like this are spotted by passing birds and recognised by them as being associated with water. I have even seen a band of long-tailed tits staying awhile as they searched for insects among swaying stems.

The great reedmace (*Typha latifolia*) will grow comfortably in water 30 centimetres in depth and produce cotton-tufted seeds from its chocolate-brown flower spikes in June and August. As a bird plant it fulfils a neutral role, except for its attractive flower and reed-like growth which typifies a wild pond. The lesser reedmace (*Typha angustifolia*) is in many ways a smaller version of the previous plant, but both form dense mats of roots growing outwards into the open water of the pond.

A pretty little plant fond of shallow water is the amphibious bistort (*Polygonum amphibium*), a member of the dock family; it sends up pinkish-coloured flowerheads that rise 15–30 centimetres out of the water from July to September. It is worth growing both for the flowers and for its leaves.

Some years ago I salvaged a plant that had been dug out of a drainage ditch in Somerset and transferred it to our pond where it thrived and produced lovely pale violet flowers scattered over a tall, graceful stem. It seems to be a disappearing species, partly, I am sure, because of its vanishing peat-water habitats. It is the common water plantain (*Alisma plantago-aquatica*) which is another attractive addition to the pond and, like all the semi- and submerged aquatic plants, it helps to use up those minerals that tend to make the water green with algae.

I have saved until the last what I consider to be quite the best of the marshy marginal plants. It is the lovely marsh marigold or kingcup (*Caltha palustris*) whose massed, bright yellow flowers glow like tiny suns in the shade of a willow tree at

Table 5. Flowering periods of water plants.

FLOWER	Feb	Mar	April	May	June	July	Aug	Sept	Oct
Marsh Marigold		<-------	---------	---------	------->				
Bogbean				<-------	------->				
Water Soldier					<-------	---------	------->		
Purple Loosestrife					<-------	---------	------->		
Bistort					<-------	---------	------->		
Yellow Flag					<-------	---------	------->		
Arrowhead						<-------	------->		
Water Plantain					<-------	---------	------->		
Yellow Water-Lily					<-------	---------	---------	------->	
Great Willowherb						<-------	---------	------->	
Water Mint						<-------	---------	------->	
Hornwort						<-------	---------	------->	

A few of the water plants to brighten your bird bathing and drinking pond.

the pond's edge in springtime. It deserves its place if for no other reason than that to see it in flower is to know with certainty that spring has arrived. To be able to watch a blackbird bathing and spraying water drops against a backdrop of kingcups is a very satisfying experience and no bird pond should be without it.

Moving out into the shallow water we come to the true aquatic plants, and if you feel you would like to include one or perhaps two water-lilies, then I suggest you try either the white water-lily (*Nymphaea alba*) or the yellow water-lily (*Nuphar lutea*). Of the two, the yellow is by far the more attractive as it is the largest, and in many places, the commonest floating yellow flower. Often with leaves a foot across, I have seen many a small bird alight on them and many a bee and wasp crawl to the edge to sup water. The white water-lily has quite fragrant flowers with a central crown of golden stamens and large floating leaves. These leaves act as shades and in cutting down the sunlight also help in algae prevention.

Both white and yellow grow from rhizomes and these should be planted in a plastic planting basket or tied lightly into a plastic net bag of good humus-rich soil which is allowed to sink gently to the bottom of the pond. Should you prefer to go for the more exotic cultivated lilies there is a wide variety of bright colours to choose from. However, in my experience, keeping to natural wild plants and copying a wild, green pond looks better and, I am quite convinced, attracts more birds.

Another valuable aquatic is Canadian pondweed (*Elodea canadensis*). All you need to start it off is a few stems and if you tie them lightly together, attach a stone as a weight and put a few into the pond, nature will do the rest. It tends to lose much of its leafy abundance in winter, but a year after planting it will practically fill the pond.

Short lengths of stem, say 18 centimetres long, can be broken off an established plant and placed where needed. These will quickly produce rootlets which grow downwards into the bottom mud and anchor the new plant.

Water milfoil (*Myriophyllum* spp) with its feathery leaf-whorls is another attractive aquatic but try and avoid the duckweeds (*Lemna* spp). Their corn-seed-sized leaves very soon blanket a pond surface and will interfere with birds bathing. It is difficult for a bird to find a patch of clear water once duckweed is established, and indeed I have yet to see a bird bathe in water where this persistent little floating plant flourishes—no doubt due to the fact that it would adhere to their feathers.

Another problem caused by duckweed is the reduction of oxygenation. In any pond, the great proportion of aeration takes place at the surface where the water is in contact with the air. Aeration proceeds most rapidly when that surface water is on the move and the wind does this quite effectively. If the surface is smothered by duckweed all movement is reduced and contact with the air prevented. It also filters out the sunlight and prevents the submerged plants growing.

Water mint (*Mentha aquatica*) is an excellent little plant to grow along the marshy edge of your pond. It should be grown exclusively for the lovely, refreshing scent given off by its leaves. It is a spreading plant and quickly permeates many of the others, but this is prevented by surrounding it with a buried metal wall so that its reproductive shoots are confined. Another obvious method is to cut through these shoots and uproot them *at least every autumn*.

Opposite: *It takes two to three years for a pond to become well established, but throughout its maturing period birds will come to drink and bathe. Maintenance is minimal, but the rewards very satisfying as the birds flock in.*

5
NEST-BUILDING TIME

Most of us must surely recall that magical moment when we were young and saw our first bird's nest, and even as we grow older the sight of a nest stimulates our senses and sets the mind to work. How they cast their spell over young and old defies simple explanation, as does the delight expressed by young children as they 'make a nest' among their toys. It was Edward Thomas, countryman and poet of rural England, who wrote:

> The summer nests uncovered by autumn wind,
> Some torn, others dislodged, all dark,
> Everyone sees them: low or high in tree,
> Or hedge, or single bush, they hang like a mark.

And so it will ever be, for it is after leaf-fall that we most easily see them, although the frenzied activity that produced such delicate structures took place when those same leaves were breaking bud. Yet with a measure of careful observation in our own garden we can enjoy both the prelude to nest-making and the first act of building, and for the finale, watch the departure of the fledglings.

A NESTING BLACKBIRD

Quite recently our garden provided a wonderful example of nesting habits by one of our commonest birds, the blackbird. For several years the pair had nested in our garden, always choosing a safe, well-hidden secure site. But this time they defied all normal precautions and decided to build on the branch of a wistaria that grew against the south-west facing wall of our patio. This site was within a metre of a door constantly used by our springer spaniel, who quickly spotted what was going on and who, despite our 'training', constantly harassed them. Nest-building began in mid-March and it was the female who did most of the building, although the male did help occasionally; but both of them, although frightened off several times a day, returned again and again. Eventually she laid four eggs. Then one early morning there was a fearful hubbub from amongst the wistaria and I got to the window just in time to see a cat beating a hasty retreat along the branch, scolded by two very irate blackbirds. Despite such a scare the female returned and steadfastly continued incubating, protected by an anti-cat barrier we hastily erected. Eight days later came a thunderstorm. Battered by large hailstones and then bombarded by a downpour, unprotected by the few early leaves, she fled. On her return she found the nest flooded and partially destroyed; finally she abandoned it. To us it was obvious that a nest in such an exposed site was doomed from the start and there seems little doubt that the blackbird was accident-prone. Yet next year she returned to nest in the garden and more 'wisely' chose an escallonia bush, where she built and successfully reared her family.

Blackbirds, generally speaking, like to build their nests some one-and-a-half to two metres high, supported by a branch and against a wall. A variety of bushes will be used—loganberry, escallonia, forsythia, and a vast number of other garden bushes as long as they are reasonably dense and backed by a wall or very thick undergrowth. In fact blackbirds build in an extraordinary number of different sites and they usually display great initiative in using anything that provides safety from predators and reasonable protection from rain and sun. But wherever a bird builds it must have a secure foundation and it is intriguing to ponder on how the bird decides the exact spot. What combination of factors determines that 'here, in this spot, the nest will be built'? Most surely a psychological factor is involved! The shape of one or more of the branches, their angle; the position of a small crutch between branches; a small projection on which to secure the first foundation; a host of such small choices has to be made before the first piece of nest material is fixed in place.

Most of the grass, moss and other material is damp when collected, indeed it seems dampness is preferred, and whilst the cause of the dampness may seem obvious—since spring rains are frequent—there is perhaps a sound reason for this preference. Damp grass stems, twigs and leaves are much more supple for the bird to manipulate into the rounded shape required and as they dry they become fixed in the curved form and are thus springy and make a stronger structure.

Quite frequently, when the nest is being built close to a wall, much of the material used, especially small twigs, is actually stuck to the wall with daubed mud. Similarly the base is often secured by mud to the branches or ledge on which it rests. Again, it is obvious that moist mud, used in the base, nest rim and for general strengthening, is plastic and amenable to fashioning, whereas dry mud would simply fall away.

Most of the nest material is gathered and carried by the female blackbird and some idea of the effort expended may be appreciated when it is realised that as much as 300 to 400 grams of damp material has to be conveyed to the site by a bird weighing around 90 grams—three to five times its own body weight, and involving perhaps as many as five hundred to a thousand individual journeys!

On average a blackbird spends three to four days making and securing the base of its nest and a further ten to twelve days completing it. Often the bird will start work quite early in the morning but take a break well before midday.

The activity involved is amazing, for the bird has to fly to a site, seek the material, then tug, pull and generally release a beakful of what is often wet and soggy vegetation; a quick flight back to the nest area where the bird usually alights on a vantage point, presumably to check that no predators are about; then a quick dart to the nest site where the load is pushed, probed, pulled and twisted into the desired position by the bird rotating and spinning amidst much bobbing. A very brief glance around, then off again to find more building material. Amidst this frenzied activity the bird has to find time to search for food, bathe and preen.

During this period it has to keep a wary eye open, its hearing tuned in to the many sounds in the garden and constantly filtering these sounds to distinguish threat from other harmless activity. The bird will no doubt very soon recognise the members of your household and in a small way 'classify' the noise from children as opposed to the more leisurely daily movements of older members of the family. It will quickly sort out how near it is safe to let you approach; that an armful of washing is harmless but that the sleeping dog needs to be kept at a distance.

I doubt if any of us is able to think like a bird, and even if many of its activities are instinctive, there is a great deal more to a bird than triggered responses to a given stimulus. Make no mistake: a bird is acutely conscious of nearly everything happening within its habitat; for certain it is, our garden blackbird knows far more about me and my activities than I shall ever learn about its life-style.

But to return to the nest-making.

For blackbirds in the garden there is a wide choice of available materials, but careful examination of what is selected reveals that most frequently used are the following: dried grass leaves and stems (especially Yorkshire fog and timothy), grass roots, small twigs of many kinds, dry, reedy leaves of montbretia, leaves of stock, cerastium, the twisty stems and leaves of aubrieta, pieces of cupressus species, skeletonised leaves, skeletonised petals of hydrangea, fuchsia leaves and bark, escallonia leaves, a few spiders' webs, and indeed a great assortment of bits and pieces of garden plants. Nearly all of these stems and twigs have small projections or are partially spiralled or have a number of tiny offshoots. From a structural viewpoint these give added strength to the finished nest. Some foundations consist of grass stems and roots, often covered with, for example, fuchsia bark, whilst others use mud to secure the base to a branch.

An interesting aspect of blackbirds' nests is the manner in which grass stems are twined around the inside circumference of the cup whilst long leaves or stems are woven in from rim to base and up to the opposite rim. All this interwoven work is then fixed together with more mud.

Mosses are gathered to be incorporated in the cup or pushed firmly into the mud around the rim. A typical species of moss so used is rough-stalked feather moss (*Brachythecium rutabulum*), a moss so common in gardens as to be almost a weed among the mosses. It is the moss most commonly used by garden birds (see p. 102). Another species used is the long-trailing feather moss (*Eurhynchium praelongum*) which grows up to 15 centimetres in length and which is found in tangled patches in gardens. Why these species are used is by no means easy to tell, but perhaps, like so many materials collected by nesting birds, they simply collect what is most obviously available, although suitability to purpose must be an important factor in choice.

GARDEN WEIGHT-LIFTERS

Moist, plastic mud is used by the song thrush to make a cup lining fashioned by the bird's constantly turning body until it is a smooth and perfect plastering job.

downy feather

moss

roots

lichen

dry leaves

mud

dry grass

skeleton leaf

hair and fur

spider's web

twigs

bark

Common nest materials.
Whilst a great variety of both organic and inorganic materials are used in different nests,
the ones illustrated here are the most commonly used.

Swallows make their nest almost entirely of pellets of mud collected from pondside and ditch so that it adheres together to become sufficiently homogeneous to stick to the wall and to form the nest itself. In each case, the mud will slowly dry out and so gain considerable strength. So it is that moisture adds a considerable weight to the nest-making materials carried by the birds. Table 6 shows the 'wet' weight of a few nests of garden birds; the figures are not averages, but taken from many records I have kept over the years.

Table 6. Weight of moist nest material relative to birds' weight.

BIRD	TOTAL WEIGHT OF NEST MATERIAL MOIST	WEIGHT OF BIRD
Blackbird	406 g	91 g
Song Thrush	282 g	87 g
House Sparrow	81 g	27 g
Robin	75 g	19 g
Dunnock	39 g	16 g
Blue Tit	35 g	12 g
Goldfinch	31 g	16 g
Swallow	One nest examined weighed (moist) 350 g. Weight of 10 individual pellets of mud 7.1 g, i.e. weight of average pellet approx. 0.7 g.	19 g

From this table it can be seen that, according to species, a bird may carry anything from one-and-a-half to four-and-a-half times its own weight of nest material from the garden to the nest site. These facts are not offered as having any scientific value, but rather so that you, as an interested observer, may gain just a little more understanding of what your garden nester is involved in. To a small bird, the light nest we handle is quite a different matter and involves considerable effort. But anyone who has handled a bird's nest is soon aware of its springy, resilient nature which gives it strength and durability and also provides insulation. All this helps to account for the number of nests that persist throughout a winter's hard weather and why we see so many in the bare outlines of hedgerow bushes. They are great survivors.

In keeping with their species size, birds are remarkably consistent in the size of their nest cups. Some species such as blackbird, blue tit, wren and house sparrow have quite a range of overall width, yet their cup sizes remain within two or three centimetres of the mean for the species. Table 7 provides a few examples taken from garden birds' nests.

Variation in size frequently occurs in 'unusual' nest sites. For example, a wren built in between the open strands of some rope coiled and hung from a beam, and the nest shape fitted closely within—and slightly over-lapping—to preserve stability. On the other hand, a wren's nest in a hole in a bank will be of quite a different shape. Blue tits in nest boxes nearly always build out to the walls of the box and so produce a square nest, although the cup is still the normal size and

Table 7. Nest measurements.
Below are listed a few sample nest dimensions. The figures represent averages and have been rounded off to the nearest half-centimetre. All measurements are in centimetres.

SPECIES	TOTAL DIAM.	CUP DIAM.	WALL THICKNESS	TOTAL DEPTH	CUP DEPTH
Blackbird	16.0	9.5	3.0	8.5	6.0
Blue Tit	9.5	5.5	2.0	5.5	4.0
Dunnock	12.5	7.0	3.0	6.5	3.5
Goldfinch	8.7	5.0	2.5	4.5	3.0
Great Tit	14.0	7.5	4.0	6.0	5.0
Greenfinch	11.5	7.0	2.5	6.0	3.0
Pied Wagtail	10.0	7.0	1.5	5.5	4.0
Robin	12.0	5.0	2.5	6.5	3.5
Song Thrush	16.0	9.5	3.0	8.0	5.5
Spotted Flycatcher	10.0	6.0	2.5	4.5	4.0
Chaffinch	9.0	6.5	2.0	6.0	5.5
Wren	15.5 × 12.0 (outside dimensions)				

shape. In a hollow tree, the same tit may well build a rounded or oval nest to conform to the limits imposed by the hollow. Some blackbirds' nests, when built tight against a wall within the rigid framework of a shrub, may be somewhat oval, yet the little goldfinch produces an almost regular rounded nest, due almost entirely to the bird sticking to its particular preference of nest site. And then again the robin, whilst favouring a normal cup-shaped nest, will often build a domed nest if it is to be situated in a hole or overgrown bank, and even the use of a short approach tunnel has been reported.

Until you become familiar with finding nests, it is remarkable how difficult they are to discover. Rather than searching trees and bushes it is far better to sit quietly and watch the behaviour of the birds. If they are building you will see them carrying materials to the site; if they have young, their frequent journeyings to and fro with food are even easier to see. Blackbirds are quite noisy, both when arriving and when leaving the nest, and when approaching will usually alight on a particular branch before flying in to the nest site; blue tits, whilst foraging in different directions, usually have two or three lines of approach and these too are quite easy to observe. But remember, birds are *always* cautious and as an observer it is essential to sit quietly, still, and remain as inconspicuous as possible.

WHO DOES THE WORK?

As can be seen by reference to Table 8, responsibility for nest-building is some-

94 THE WILD BIRD GARDEN

Table 8. Preparation and caring for the young

SPECIES	NEST BUILDING RESPONSIBILITIES ♀	♂	INCUBATION OF EGGS ♀	♂	FEEDING AND FLEDGLINGS / FEEDING NESTLINGS ♀	♂	FLEDGING PERIOD – DAYS	NUMBER OF BROODS	INCUBATION PERIOD – DAYS	NUMBER OF EGGS
Blackbird	X	occ X	X		X	X	12–15	2–3	12–15	3–5
Blue Tit	X	X	X		X	X	19+	1	14	7–16
Bullfinch	X		X		X	X	12–16	2	12–14	4–5
Chaffinch	X		X		X	X	13–14	1	11–13	4–5
Coal Tit	X	X	X		X	X	c16	1–s2	c14	7–11
Collared Dove	X	X	X	X	X	X	21	2–3+	14	2
Dunnock	X		X		X	X	12	2–3	12	4–5
Goldfinch	X		X		X	X	13–15	2–s3	12–13	5–6
Great Tit	X	X	X		X	X	19	1	12–16	5–12
Greenfinch	X		X		X	X	13–16	2–s3	13–14	4–6
House Martin	X	X	X	X	X	X	10–22	2–3	14	4–5
House Sparrow	X	X	X	occ X	X	X	11–19	1–4	9–18	3–6
Long-Tailed Tit	X	X	X	occ X	X		15–16	1	14–18	7–12
Pied Wagtail	X		X	v.occ X	X	X	14–16	2–s3	13–14	5–6
Robin	X		X		X	X	12–15	2–s3	12–14	5–7
Song Thrush	X		X		X	X	12–15	2–3	12–14	3–5
Spotted Flycatcher	X	X	X	X	X	X	12–15	1–2	12–14	4–5
Starling	X	X	X	X	X	X	20–22	1–s2	12–13	4–7
Wren	X	X	X		X	occ X	16–17	2	14–15	5–6

+ denotes 'or more' v.occ denotes 'very occasional'
c denotes 'about' occ denotes 'occasional'
s denotes 'sometimes'

Acknowledgements to Bruce Campbell and James Ferguson-Lees for permission to use material in the columns on fledging, broods, incubation and eggs from their book *A Field Guide to Birds' Nests* (Constable, 1972).

Pied wagtail about to enter nest in hanging basket. Birds sometimes nest in unexpected places and you will need to be observant to discover them. This wagtail reared five young despite daily watering disturbance.

times shared, while in some species either male or female does the work. Of *nineteen* birds quite commonly found nesting in gardens, duties are performed as follows:

Female involved in nest building	19
Male involved in nest building	5
Male sometimes accompanies female	11

From these figures it can be plainly seen that the female, without exception, is the main nest builder. Only very occasionally does the male help out with the building although he often watches her collect the material and flies back to the nest site where he stands by as she does the weaving. No doubt his main function is to guard their territory, and whilst his singing from the tree top may seem a lot easier than carrying all that nest material, he is performing an equally important role.

Later on, when the young hatch out, he certainly does his share in the feeding.

Table 9. Main period of eggs and young for some garden birds.

	Jan	Feb	Mar	April	May	June	July	Aug	Sept	Oct	Nov
Collared Dove	‹·	······	··· ---	-------	-------	-------	-------	-------	---- ··	······	···›
Robin				‹--------	-------	-------	····›				
Song Thrush		‹···	··· ---	-------	-------	-------	------- ···›				
Dunnock				‹--------	-------	-------	------›				
House Sparrow				‹-------	-------	-------	------- ------›				
Long-Tailed Tit				‹-----------------›							
Starling				‹-------	-------	------›					
Blue Tit				‹-------	-------	------›					
Blackbird				‹----	-------	------›					
Chaffinch				‹---	-------	------›					
Coal Tit				‹----	-------	-----›					
Pied Wagtail				‹----	-------	-------	------- ---›				
Wren				‹----	-------	-------	-----›				
Great Tit				‹-	-------	-----›					
Greenfinch				‹-	-------	-------	------- ······ ···›				
House Martin					‹----	-------	-------	-------	-------- -›		
Spotted Flycatcher					‹---	-------	------- -----›				

NEST BOXES

In the wild, hole-nesters need to seek out not only a suitable hollow tree but also one with a reasonably-sized entrance hole. The problem that arises is simply that when the hole is too large for, say, a pair of blue tits, then larger species like the starling may appropriate it whilst the smaller pair are building. Nevertheless, few hole-nesters will find a site with a hole of the diameter advised in most nest box guides. The more precise sizes are suggested as being ideals, the near-perfect dimensions for comfortable nesting.

In the wild, too, birds will seek hollow trees that are dry. An opening on the upper side of a slightly sloping tree will collect all the rainwater run-off, whereas an opening on the underside will be drier. Height of nest site is also an important factor. It is a remarkable fact that most trees tend to lose branches at least two metres above ground level and higher, and these breakages rot and form the holes. The depth and general all-round dimensions of the hollow will also be extremely variable, whereas in custom-made boxes the sizes have been refined down by experience.

Because we frequently hear of unusual nest sites, there is a tendency to believe that measurements are not too important, but whilst in gardens the choice for positioning home-produced boxes may be very limited, it is worth trying to adhere to the general principles researched by organisations such as RSPB, BTO and Nature Conservancy.

Next let us consider the material to be used. When you visit your DIY store or timber yard ask for unplaned wood, sometimes referred to as rough-cut or rough-sawn. Ask if they have any wood that has been treated with a preservative. If you are fortunate there may be one or two kinds of wood available, such as hardwoods like oak or softwoods like cedar, but whichever one you decide on check that it is free from splits, holes or cracks. Most amusing of all will be to see the expression on the merchant's face when you ask for well-seasoned wood. These days timber seems to come out of the ground and reach the suppliers almost with the leaves still on, and the consequent drying process occasions all sorts of distortions in the finished product. Slightly more expensive and not always obtainable in smaller sizes (usual sheets are 2440 mm by 1220 mm) is marine ply. This is absolutely the best weather-resistant wood but it is better to rough up the inside and front surfaces to provide toe-holds for the birds.

Plank width for smaller birds such as blue and great tits, pied flycatcher and starling should be 150 mm and for a larger bird like a stock dove, 200 mm. I prefer a 19 mm thickness of plank as it gives more latitude in fixing screws; 13 mm is rather thin and takes more skill in assembly.

Incidentally, if you decide to use creosote or solignum or any painted-on preservative, give it a couple of months to weather and rid itself of smells.

Having got the wood you will need means of fixing it together. Since the bird box should be in position for many seasons, use the best you can afford. Brass screws are by far the best as they do not rust and cause rot to develop around the screw holes. Nails can be used but inevitably warping may occur as nails do not

have the bonding strength of a good brass screw. Similarly, hinges should be of brass, and go for strong ones too. Steel hinges will eventually seize up and fall apart. Plastic hinges are reasonably good but these too have a limited life because their metal shaft rusts out.

Marking out and assembly

For a typical tit box, mark out the plank as explained in the diagram overleaf.

When assembling, it is a good plan to use a waterproof glue such as Evostick wood glue (waterproof), or one of the Bostik waterproof wood glues. This will not only make a stronger finished job but will prevent water-creep through the joints.

Entrance holes

These may be placed on either side or at the front. Again, reference to the recommended guides will give the best sizes, but a few typical examples are:

Great tits	28 mm	Pied flycatcher	28 mm
Blue tits	25 mm	House sparrow	32 mm

If the holes are 'attacked' by woodpeckers seeking to enlarge the entrances for themselves, you would be wise to tack a piece of tin plate (a piece from a soup tin will do nicely) over the hole, having first cut a hole of the required size to match the wooden one. Paint both sides of the tin to discourage rusting.

To protect the hinged lid thoroughly, waterproof material should be tacked over the hinges, as the crack where the lid meets the back is always a potential source of rain seepage.

Fixing the nest box

It is most important to secure the box so that it will not vibrate or wobble, even in a gale. If you are fixing it to a tall pole or substantial tree, the top and bottom screws must be thoroughly tight. Fix it at least two metres above ground and anywhere up to four metres. In so doing make sure it is sloping slightly, with the entrance pointing down and *not* up. Try to fix it where direct midday sun does not fall on it. It is a good idea to choose a site where sheltering branches shade the nest box and also provide perching for a bird flying in with food. A bird usually arrives and perches a few yards away from the nest, ensures all is safe and then alights on the box, usually toe-holding the lower edge of the hole. A perching stick attached to the box 25 mm or so below the hole is included in many designs, but is far from necessary.

There is a host of designs available, but quite the best are in two reliable

Opposite: *Blue tit in nest box.*
According to where you live the dates of egg-laying can vary considerably. Some will have nestlings among the apple blossom and others not until the June roses begin to flower.
Try to understand the constant effort needed to feed these nestlings. They have almost insatiable appetites.

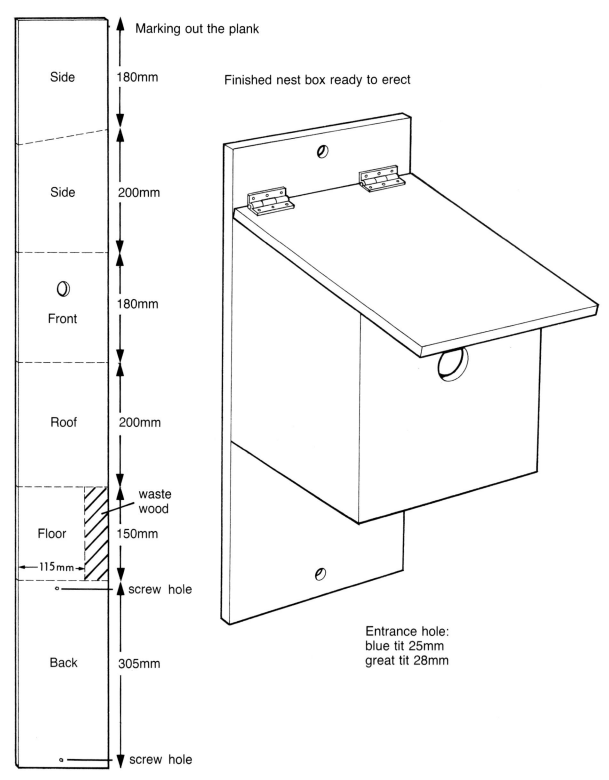

Marking out the plank

Side   180mm

Side   200mm

Front   180mm

Roof   200mm

Floor   150mm

waste wood

115mm

screw hole

Back   305mm

screw hole

150mm × 19mm plank

Finished nest box ready to erect

Entrance hole:
blue tit 25mm
great tit 28mm

guides—*Nestboxes*, Field Guide No. 3 by J.J.M. Flegg and D.E. Glue, and BTO Guide No. 20 *Nestboxes* (6th ed), by Chris du Feu. Both are published by the British Trust for Ornithology.

Since birds have become a minor industry some rather startling designs have been appearing in the shops. But birds do not look for little summer houses, cottages and imitation tree trunks in gaudy plastic; they much prefer good old-fashioned wood from their own environment.

As the owner of a nest box you have an important duty towards your visitors. Remember *always* that their relaxation and safety must come first, so any lifting of the lid should be kept to the absolute minimum. By careful observation you should be able to estimate the best time for a look inside and do it when both parents are away from the nest. Never, repeat never, open a box within a few days of when the fledglings are due to fly. Such disturbance usually results in a minor explosion of young out into the dangerous world where, alas, most will die. Personally I *never* look inside the nest box but prefer to enjoy all the activity that goes on outside.

Nest box cleaning

Some time after the young have flown—and it is always as well to allow for a second or even third brood—the old nest should be removed and the box thoroughly cleaned. Autumn, around late September or early October, is the best time to do it. The reason for getting rid of the used nest is the hundreds of bird fleas that remain in the structure. A good dusting with pyrethrum should destroy the few that have got into corners and small cracks. Having finished the cleaning, check hinges, joints and woodwork and carry out any repairs necessary.

Beware predators

Site the nest box so that cats cannot climb up to it. That is not as easy as it sounds: cats display amazing ingenuity at reaching birds' nests in garden situations.

Providing you have set your nest box in place in late summer or early autumn, all you now have to do is wait—hopefully. Keep an eye on the site from early January onwards, especially when one of those winter high pressure systems brings winds from the south and sunny blue skies. The earliest record in our garden revealed a blue tit looking *out* of the nest box on 13 January. She was obviously the female, and fluttering around the lime tree branches was her attendant male, busy cheeping and quite obviously excited. After a prolonged series of gales and endless rain, that sunny January day had heightened the seasonal rhythms in their tiny bodies and brought a touch of spring into their lives. Such early prospecting does not mean they are nest-building, but as the house agent you have had a desirable property to let and now the 'sold' notice can go up!

Opposite: *Making a nest box. Entrance hole sizes should be accurate, but the actual size of the box is less important. The measurements indicated have proved successful, but there is still room for experiment in general nest box construction. The design given here is adapted from* Nestboxes (BTO Guide 20) by Chris du Feu *and* Nestboxes (Field Guide 3), *both BTO Publications, by permission of British Trust for Ornithology.*

MOSSES—A FEW COMMON SPECIES USED IN NEST-BUILDING

Whilst there is no need for the bird gardener to identify mosses, there is always interest in discovering a little more about a bird's requirements. Generally speaking, most of the mosses used tend to be the bushy or long, feathered species and not those that cling closely to rock, fence, soil or tree. Presumably a bird goes for the larger and longer ones as they offer better potential for nest-building, and a very large proportion of the more popularly used species are at least up to 15 centimetres in length (see Table 10).

Urban nests

In nests from semi-urban gardens that I have examined, one of the mosses most commonly used is rough-stalked feather moss (*Brachythecium rutabulum*). This is one of the most common and abundant feather mosses to be found in gardens where it is frequently regarded as a weed, due to its habit of forming extensive carpets in damp, shady places. It is a bright, shiny green and will be found on walls, bare soil hedgebanks and rocks. Left well alone and occasionally watered in spells of dry weather, it will flourish and hopefully prove a valuable asset to garden birds busy nest-building.

Long-trailing feather moss (*Eurhynchium praelongum*) often grows in tangled patches in gardens and at the base of woodland trees. Its long, creeping main stems make it an ideal material for weaving among grasses during nest construction.

Pale-trailing feather moss (*Eurhynchium swartzii*) is very common on chalky soils and often grows in a mixed community with the previous species. Shade-loving, it is found growing on decaying logs and on turf away from the sun.

Cypress-leaved feather moss (*Hypnum cupressiforme*) is very common on rocks, walls, trees, logs and soil. It has shoots up to 8 cm in length.

As can be seen in Table 10, other mosses used by birds include the drooping-leaved feather moss (*Rhytidiadelphus squarrosus*) which forms carpets on grassland and is frequently regarded by non bird-horticulturalists as a pest on their lawns.

Amblystegium serpens is a moss with no English name but is a slender feather moss that is abundant on wet stones, moist soil and around the base of trees. In spring its bright red spore capsules, nearly 25 mm in length, will help in its identification.

Calliergon cuspidatum is an abundant moss which grows in moist grassland and marshy ground and occasionally becomes a nuisance on otherwise well-kept lawns.

Rural nests

From examination of a few rural nests, it is mostly the woodland species that are used.

Isothecium myosuroides is a quite bushy moss which can be found growing in spreading mats on both rocks and trees, providing they are in the damp shade. An emerald-green species is the tamarisk-leaved feather moss (*Thuidium tamariscinum*) which commonly grows in woodland, again in damp shade, or occasionally in well draped hedgebanks. It grows up to 10 cm in thick mats.

Table 10. Urban nests.
Identified mosses from thirteen garden nests. Figures in brackets are personal reference nest numbers.

SPECIES	Brachythecium rutabulum	Eurhynchium praelongum	Eurhynchium swartzii	Hypnum cupressiforme	Hypnum mammillatum	Rhytidiadelphus squarrosus	Amblystegium serpens	Calliergon cuspidatum	LICHEN	Evernia prunastri
Blackbird (2)	X	X						90% X		
Blackbird (3)	X	X								
Blue Tit (1)	X							X		
Dunnock (1)	X	X	X							
Dunnock (2)	X	X	X							
Spotted Flycatcher	X			X						
Goldfinch (5)	X			X		X				
Greenfinch	X									
Pied Wagtail		X			X					X
Robin	X		X							
Sparrow A	X	X	few X				X			
Wren (4)	X	X								
Goldfinch						X				

Table 11. Rural nests.
Showing examples of mosses and liverworts used in nest construction by birds in a rural environment.

SPECIES	MOSSES						LIVERWORTS	
	Isothecium myosuroides	Hypnum andoi	Eurhynchium striatum	Thuidium tamariscinum	Eurhynchium praelongum	Rhytidiadelphus loreus	Metzgeria furcata	Frullania tamarisci
Great Tit	X		X	X	X	X		
Blue Tit	X		X					X
Spotted Flycatcher	X	X					X	X

A feather moss *Rhytidiadelphus loreus* is an upland species that favours acid-rich humus, rocks and screes, often producing stems up to 20 cm in length.

Different species of birds use moss in varying quantities (some none at all), and a bird like a blue tit, once having located a suitable moss, returns again and again. This sometimes results in a nest being composed of a single or at most two species of moss. I guess it is more direct and simpler that way.

It is interesting to note that both blue tit and spotted flycatcher used liverworts in their nest and one species, *Frullania tamarisci*, was common to both birds' nests. Liverworts generally have flattish stems and leaves and are usually found abundantly beside streams, especially where water tumbles down in waterfall fashion and sprays water around. It would be satisfying to discover why some birds choose liverworts.

The identification of mosses is a difficult task for anyone not familiar with their general biology, but a most useful book is Collins *Guide to the Ferns, Mosses and Lichens of Britain and Northern and Central Europe* by Hans Martin Jahns. Its 655 colour photographs will help you, should you decide to sort a few of them out.

6
BIRDS IN TOWN AND COUNTRY GARDENS

The British Trust for Ornithology, which is constantly engaged in discovering new facts about bird life, has recently completed a three-year fieldwork study of garden birds. During that period more than 6,000 people have been recording the birds that visited their gardens. This great effort was sponsored by BASF who gave complete financial support throughout the three years.

Lys Muirhead compiled the report and from the following details, the variations between town and country are revealed since the figures show the average percentage of gardens visited by the 'top twelve' during the autumn of 1989.

Why not watch your own garden and compare your results with the following?

Regional boundaries used in the following Bird Survey.

WHAT TO EXPECT WHERE YOU LIVE

Scotland (1)

SUBURBAN		RURAL	
Blackbird	90	Robin	92
Blue Tit	88	Blackbird	91
House Sparrow	88	Blue Tit	85
Robin	87	Chaffinch	81
Starling	81	Great Tit	76
Chaffinch	70	Dunnock	71
Great Tit	69	House Sparrow	61
Dunnock	67	Coal Tit	52
Coal Tit	51	Wren	44
Collared Dove	44	Greenfinch	43
Greenfinch	42	Starling	42
Wren	32	Song Thrush	26

Northern England (2)

SUBURBAN		RURAL	
House Sparrow	91	Blue Tit	95
Blue Tit	90	Robin	92
Blackbird	88	Blackbird	88
Starling	82	House Sparrow	85
Robin	81	Great Tit	84
Great Tit	67	Starling	75
Dunnock	67	Dunnock	75
Magpie	54	Chaffinch	65
Wren	46	Wren	59
Chaffinch	39	Coal Tit	47
Collared Dove	38	Greenfinch	46
Coal Tit	38	Magpie	46

Eastern England (3)

SUBURBAN		RURAL	
Blackbird	96	House Sparrow	95
House Sparrow	95	Blackbird	94
Starling	87	Blue Tit	90
Blue Tit	83	Starling	90
Robin	76	Robin	89
Dunnock	65	Great Tit	79
Great Tit	58	Dunnock	74
Song Thrush	58	Wren	70
Wren	47	Song Thrush	62
Greenfinch	40	Chaffinch	48
Chaffinch	28	Greenfinch	44
Collared Dove	26	Collared Dove	32

South East-England (4)

SUBURBAN		RURAL	
House Sparrow	90	Blackbird	91
Blackbird	89	Robin	91
Starling	86	Blue Tit	89
Blue Tit	85	House Sparrow	84
Robin	80	Starling	81
Great Tit	58	Great Tit	77
Dunnock	56	Dunnock	63
Magpie	52	Wren	59
Collared Dove	40	Magpie	55
Song Thrush	40	Chaffinch	54
Woodpigeon	40	Collared Dove	48
Greenfinch	40	Greenfinch	47

South-West England (5)

SUBURBAN		RURAL	
Blue Tit	88	Blue Tit	91
Robin	82	Robin	90
House Sparrow	82	Blackbird	88
Blackbird	81	Great Tit	82
Starling	78	House Sparrow	78
Great Tit	64	Chaffinch	75
Chaffinch	55	Starling	69
Dunnock	52	Wren	68
Magpie	50	Dunnock	66
Collared Dove	50	Magpie	54
Wren	47	Greenfinch	53
Greenfinch	40	Collared Dove	50

Central England (6)

SUBURBAN		RURAL	
House Sparrow	94	Blue Tit	93
Blue Tit	92	Robin	89
Blackbird	86	Blackbird	86
Starling	82	Great Tit	82
Robin	80	House Sparrow	82
Dunnock	68	Starling	71
Great Tit	68	Dunnock	67
Magpie	51	Wren	60
Wren	48	Chaffinch	60
Collared Dove	44	Magpie	56
Coal Tit	43	Collared Dove	47
Chaffinch	38	Greenfinch	43

SUBURBAN		RURAL		SUBURBAN		RURAL	
Wales (7)				*Northern Ireland (8)*			
House Sparrow	87	Blue Tit	93	Blue Tit	87	Robin	95
Blue Tit	87	Robin	92	House Sparrow	84	Blue Tit	81
Robin	86	Blackbird	81	Robin	80	Chaffinch	85
Starling	77	Chaffinch	84	Starling	80	Starling	76
Great Tit	72	Great Tit	80	Chaffinch	71	House Sparrow	75
Blackbird	72	Magpie	67	Blackbird	69	Blackbird	75
Chaffinch	62	Wren	65	Coal Tit	58	Great Tit	68
Magpie	58	House Sparrow	60	Magpie	52	Wren	67
Dunnock	50	Dunnock	59	Great Tit	57	Dunnock	64
Wren	50	Coal Tit	46	Dunnock	44	Magpie	59
Coal Tit	49	Starling	45	Collared Dove	42	Coal Tit	49
Collared Dove	47	Greenfinch	44	Greenfinch	40	Rook	49

Acknowledgements to the BTO and BTO/BASF Garden Bird Survey Newsletter, September 1990.

BLACKBIRD *(Turdus merula)*. Merle, Ousel, Woosel Cock

There must be few gardens without a familiar blackbird and even fewer that never hear its alarm call as the male flings itself out of a bush when disturbed by the local cat. Sometimes it chooses to remain in cover uttering its loud ticking call, but that is only when threat is remote and it feels safer in hiding.

Best of all is its delightful song, a liquid fluting, called to the sky from the bird's favourite perch near the top of a tree. From mid-March onwards most gardens are embellished by this lovely song.

The female blackbird is dark brown above and rufous-brown below, with dark mottling. Some females have a quite distinctive whitish throat, which has been known to cause some people to assume the visit of a ring-ousel. Indeed, partially white blackbirds are not at all uncommon, and these too can lead to unnecessary excitement that a new species is on the lawn.

Juveniles are often much lighter than the females and, with their more pronounced mottling, may be confused with song thrushes.

In winter, our compost heap, well sprinkled with the remains of autumn's apples, is often 'taken over' by our resident blackbird who defends his food source against all comers. Even the fieldfares, flying in on the snow, defer to his possessive instinct.

Blackbirds enjoy plenty of cover, especially when there is an abundance of dead leaves on the soil, harbouring so many small insects and crustaceans. Spend a little while watching the bird back-kicking the leaves as it searches and, incidentally, try to discover whether the blackbird in your garden is left-footed, right-footed or both-footed. Some birds show a definite preference for one foot over another.

In favourable seasons you will see the male territory-holder attacking intruders, and as they are often early nesters this chasing can begin in December. Details of their nesting habits are discussed in Chapter 5.

The food of blackbirds is extremely varied and they enjoy a range of berries, fruits, worms, caterpillars, spiders, insects, snails and slugs. Earlier today I watched a male blackbird pecking off the orange berries of our *Pyracantha rogersiana*—eleven in less than two minutes. It fed neatly and decisively, pausing only to select the next beakful. The highest density of these birds occurs in suburban areas, no doubt in part due to the gardens which offer both food and suitable nesting places.

It is a very attractive bird which, in addition to providing that very mellow accompaniment to the other sounds of a summer evening, frequently enlivens the autumn and winter garden with its busy, bustling and excitable behaviour.

BLUE TIT *(Parus caeruleus)*. Tom-tit, Blue Titmouse, Billy-biter, Ackymal
Surely one of the most attractive little birds to visit our gardens, and fortunately most gardens have some tits at some time during the year.

Dr Christopher Perrins, in his classic book *British Tits*, writes:

> The more we learn about them, the more involved their lives are seen to be. For example we realise that in their search for food they are not just dashing hither and thither through the trees, but are searching in a complex and highly non-random manner . . . Whether we are 'scientific' and regard them as having a 'large number of adaptive responses', or are anthropomorphic and look on them as 'clever', their lives are extraordinarily intricate.

Their natural habitat is in broad-leaved deciduous woodland, and in particular they favour oak woods. In my area of south-west England we are fortunate in having some fine oak woodlands and if you walk through one of these at any time of the year you will see a number of blue tits busy feeding among the foliage. There, in those leafy pastures in spring and summer, vast numbers of caterpillars browse away, small spiders hunt the flies that come to feed on the honeydew released from millions of aphids, whilst weevils, beetles, gall wasps and wood ants live out their lives until seized by a hunting blue tit.

Most small insectivorous birds tap an enormous variety of natural resources, based on all the different woodland features of leaf, gall, twig, fruit, epiphytic growth on bough and trunk, fungi and dead wood . . . they explore in the course of the year every accessible food that can be utilised, wandering restlessly and endlessly in their minute investigations, like shoppers in an immensely varied food store.

The blue tit's acrobatic behaviour at your bird table is the natural result of hours spent hanging from tiny twigs, bending upside-down to examine the underside of leaves and twisting and turning into almost inaccessible tree offerings. Bearing in mind that much of the tree is in constant motion we can better appreciate the blue tit's 'fidgety quick' behaviour. It is one reason why hanging food is so popular and why, no matter how hard the wind blows, this little bird will alight and feed on your swinging peanuts. It just comes naturally.

In an oak wood in spring, just about the time of bud-burst and on into early summer, a quartet of moths undergo a population explosion.

The winter moth (*Operophtera brumata*), green oak moth (*Tortrix viridiana*), mottled umber (*Erannis defoliaria*) and the spring usher (*Erannis leucophaeria*), provide the eggs that produce an army of caterpillars which occupy the woodland canopy. And for the tits they provide a time of plenty. Considering a well-nourished blue tit weighs a little more than twelve grams, and bearing in mind that both cock and hen work together to build the nest, each little bird must carry its own weight in material to the site—for the dry nest weighs between 25 and 32 grams. Since much of the nest material is damp when gathered, the weight carried may be half as much again. And it is not just a question of weight because the birds have to search to find the materials, fly to and fro to collect and deliver and still find time for feeding and preening. No wonder blue tits are busy from dawn to dusk in the breeding season and nearly as long in the cold winter when food is scarce.

Large quantities of moss (see p. 102) are used in the nest and many pieces of dried grass leaves incorporated within the massed moss. The cup of the nest is very neat and quite small, about 5.5 cm in diameter with a 2 cm wall, and the cup itself only 4 cm deep. This cup is completely padded with soft hairs of different kinds, the whole woven and shaped to form a thick, soft and springy felted wall. Some of the nests have a few downy feathers within the cup and the whole inside feels extremely soft to the touch.

All birds need to have their actual nest cup of a certain size, but in the case of hole-nesters the outer dimensions are extremely variable. Obviously a small cavity offers less scope for extra surrounding nest material than a large one; a nest box varies from natural tree cavities. So unlike the birds that build in the open and can therefore maintain a regular shape and size, the hole-nesters have to be more adaptable. And the blue tit is certainly that.

In winter blue tits will often feed in flocks in the oak woods, and to watch their activity on a quiet winter's day adds much to the pleasure of a woodland afternoon.

From its life in its natural habitat it can be seen that a garden with plenty of tree cover and hedging bushes provides a semi-natural habitat that will attract this little bird.

BULLFINCH *(Pyrrhula pyrrhula)*

This attractive bird has, unfortunately, unattractive habits, being exceptionally fond of fruit buds. Every spring these birds visit commercial orchards and rip out the blossom bud, and the consequent loss of crop proves almost disastrous. Plum and pear are most vulnerable, followed by gooseberries and currants, then apples and cherries. Such attacks begin as early as November and continue through to April, as the buds of each tree species swell to an attractive size. Those garden shrubs and trees that have an even earlier bud swell, such as forsythia, are also attacked. The reason for this appears to be related to the fact that many horticultural species tend to produce swollen buds well ahead of their wild counterparts such as hawthorn. A bird of woodland and hedgerow, it has spread into domestic sites because of easy pickings. In areas where ash is plentiful and in years of high seed yield, these provide the main winter diet.

The bullfinch's bad reputation has grown in parallel with the growth of monoculture crops and the spread of orchards, pick-and-park, and other commercial outlets, without which it might well have a population cycle entwined with the varying seasonal abundance of the ash and other wild food-plants. But the presence of such an abundance of food 'offered' by human activity proves irresistible.

From April into December it feeds on all manner of wild seeds, among which is dandelion, chickweed, buttercups, charlock, dock and nettle.

Bullfinches have an interesting habit of forming, each spring, special mouth sacs on either side of the tongue, in which food is held in order to carry it back to their young.

The total bulk of food held in these sacs is comparable in size to a large cherry, and that is quite an economical way to feed nestlings. Bullfinches are not common in gardens, so you can count yourself fortunate if you have one or more. Not fond of bird tables, they will occasionally take nuts from a dispenser.

CHAFFINCH *(Fringilla coelebs)*. Bachelor Finch, Spink

Winter is the time when chaffinches come into the garden and it is then that their frequency of occurrence among the top fifteen garden birds is around 30 per cent in suburban gardens and 60 per cent in rural gardens. It is one of the commonest birds of our hedgerows where pairs frequently nest as close as three hundred metres from each other. Any closer and the territory would be too small to provide the food needed.

For much of the year the chaffinch is a seed-eater and in consequence is a very common bird on farms where it eats the various cereal grains in the heads on standing corn. After the harvest it finds a few seeds among the stubble, although two factors have come into play here. Firstly, the combine harvester takes almost 100 per cent of the seed whereas years ago stooks of corn were left standing in the field, and secondly, the burning of stubble that became so rampant in the '60s and '70s must surely have destroyed millions of seeds that might otherwise have been available throughout the winter months.

Two other factors may also be of importance. Firstly, the almost indiscriminate use of chemical seed dressings, especially the highly toxic organo-chlorine compounds, caused a rapid decline in bird numbers in the 'sixties, especially where cereals were extensively cropped. Secondly, the use of herbicides dedicated to clean, weed-free crops has meant fewer weed seeds for food and also fewer seeds left in the soil that could be gathered as winter food, especially after ploughing when dormant seeds are lifted. Many of us will recall those golden fields of wheat with the serried ranks of scarlet poppies, blue corn cockle and pale pink corn spurrey that have now disappeared. At one time it was estimated that hundreds of millions of seeds remained viable in every acre of land, but the decline in weeds produces an immediate decline in 'locked-up' seeds in the ground.

Opposite: *From midsummer until late winter bullfinches will feed on dock seeds and other weed seeds. Generally they prefer to feed by perching on the plant, rather than picking seeds off the ground. A handsome bird that may well be attracted to your garden by the seeding wild plants you have grown.*

To a small finch weighing around 22–23 grams, a constant food source is essential, and with the coming of late spring into summer there is a change of food source to a more protein-rich diet of caterpillars and varied insects caught on the ground and among tree leaves, and of flies and moths caught on the wing.

It is interesting to note that the main chaffinch nesting period is May to June — in other words, the hatching of the many nestlings coincides with the sudden population explosion of caterpillars.

The nest is usually built in a hedge, in a bush or tree, but sometimes in well-planted gardens it will build its nest in the shelter of a creeper.

Both cock, very occasionally, and hen entirely, gather the nest material but the cock leaves the hen to get on with the actual building, and a very fine and beautiful, neat and tidy nest she makes, secured as it is in the fork formed by a few branches. The neat cup is lined with feathers. The walls are composed of felted moss, thin grass stalks interwoven and thin, twisty, knobbled roots either pulled from the base of grass clumps or collected from recently ploughed land. In gardens, compost heaps often provide a source of such materials. The outer cover of the nest is plastered with lichen collected from the bark and branches of trees. Very often the branches of blackthorn accumulate growths of lichen, and where this is a common hedgerow bush, the chaffinch collects abundantly. Spiders' webs are gathered and skilfully used to bind the nest together. Thus the nest is actually composed of layers: the outside is lichen-bound with spider's web silk; then a mixed layer of interwoven moss and grass; next a layer comprised almost entirely of grass and rootlets; finally a soft feather lining.

Usually four to five eggs are laid and these are incubated by the female for up to fourteen days. Then comes the hectic feeding time to rear the nestlings which are fed by both parents. Incidentally, the newly emerged young are blind, quite unable to control their movements and barely covered with wisps of down. After the effort of raising their heads and opening beaks to receive food from the perching parent, a chick simply collapses with its head among the feathers at the base of the cup. Within a week the young are alert, able to stand up and even try to elbow each other away from presented food. Fed on a rich diet of either whole or broken pieces of caterpillar, they grow fast, begin to exercise their wings and within a fortnight have left the nest.

But still they are tended by the parents, and as the days pass they are 'encouraged' by the parents to remain in cover and if the situation is favourable are led to places where caterpillars are massed, such as occurs with many hedgerow moth species; sometimes they alight and begin to pick up seeds from ploughed land, or anywhere where seeds are likely to be lying.

Our garden chaffinches are often immigrant birds from Scandinavia, which usually arrive in autumn, between September and November. These birds leave again by early spring.

When feeding in our gardens it is usually peanuts that attract them: they are quite adept at clinging onto the nut dispensers and quickly extract what they need. They also come to bird tables where seed is, and they are not averse to feeding on a variety of scraps. But their visits can vary from year to year and you will probably notice that there are seldom more than two chaffinches feeding on your table at one time—quite unlike the swarming arrival of a pack of starling. They are birds that like space when feeding.

One vital ingredient to encourage chaffinches to nest in your garden is the provision of a singing post, a tree, from which it can proclaim territory, as can be seen and heard in the wild every springtime as the countryside's most common song accompanies your walk.

This bird is the most widespread finch in Europe and certainly the commonest in the British Isles, so one might imagine it to be frequent in all our gardens. Yet such is not always the case and many suburban gardens enjoy their visits only occasionally.

The bird's love of trees is derived from its natural woodland habitat, and whilst parks and gardens with a good spread of mature trees will attract it, flat areas of lawn and open gardens are not favoured. This is another useful pointer to the value of studying the bird's natural habitat, if we wish to attract them to our gardens. After a little while it becomes almost second nature to appreciate a bird's needs, and that understanding will contribute more than half to your success in encouraging them to visit your garden.

Coal Tit *(Parus ater)*. Cole Tit

Black cap, white patch on nape of neck and bright white cheeks distinguish this tit from the others visiting you. In the wild it has thrived in the conifer plantations that have spread across the countryside and this provides a small clue to how you might try to encourage it into your garden. By planting some conifers of the species suggested on pages 36–41, you could perhaps attract them, and the conifers anyway will be useful in offering shelter, nest and roosting sites for other species.

Coal tits feed mostly on insects during the summer months and on seeds such as beech mast, ash and spruce together with what few insects they can find, in winter. It is during the cold months, after the insects have died, hibernated, gone to ground or been eaten, that this tit visits our gardens in search of peanuts. It has the interesting habit of storing food, and if you watch one at work on the peanut dispenser you will see it extract a nut, fly off with it and return quite soon. The quickness of return usually indicates that it has been hiding the nut in the bark of a tree or in a hollow branch and so on. To what extent it finds such food when needed is a matter of conjecture, but it obviously finds enough to make the habit worth while. It is a nimble little bird and can with equal dexterity alight on a tit-bell upside-down, inspect the underside of leaves for caterpillars and other insects or search the ground for beech nuts.

Whilst I can find no report of coal tits feeding on mealworms, I suspect they may well be tempted in the early winter after their caterpillar supply dies out.

Watching the coal tits visit our peanut feeders, it became obvious that in general the birds showed definite preferences. To determine which kind of feeder they preferred in our garden we fixed three different types of feeder to hang from the bird table. One was the familiar red plastic siskin peanut bag; the other two were the typical cylindrical, square mesh feeders, one 20 cm long and the other 45 cm

Chaffinches prefer plenty of variety in their diet. Used to feeding on insects in trees, the occasional bird will land on insect-infected plants. Dahlias are prone to attack by earwigs, an invertebrate that the chaffinch enjoys. (Dahlia 'Klankstad Kerkrade'.)

long. All of them were filled to the top with peanuts and we then recorded, over a number of days, each visit made by a coal tit to these feeders. The results were:

Coal tit visits to long feeder	82 per cent
Coal tit visits to short feeder	15 per cent
Coal tit visits to 'siskin' net bag	3 per cent

In general the coal tits collected peanuts and flew off with them and seldom stayed to feed *in situ*.

COLLARED DOVE (*Streptopelia decaocto*)

There must be few gardens that have not been visited by these doves; usually they fly in pairs, coming in to feed at the bird table when it is unoccupied, or else descending on a nearby vegetable plot to pick at the young cabbage plants. They are a very successful species, especially when one considers that it was unknown in this country before 1952. It spread from India in the 1700s and is a wonderful example of a bird finding an ecological niche and taking advantage of it. 'Niche' is a convenient word used to describe the place of a bird within its environment— that is, its relationship to all other species, its food and predators. No two species could ever survive with *exactly* similar needs, for one would inevitably eliminate the other, thus creating a niche for itself.

The collared dove is a near-perfect example of a bird that found a vacant niche and has now almost fully occupied it.

In just over twenty years its numbers increased to more than twenty thousand pairs, and now it is still increasing logarithmically.

It is a species that lives very close to human habitation yet seems to be wary of our presence. For instance, a pair come regularly to our bird table but alight on the roof of the table and fidget about for a minute or more before going in to feed, and even then they seldom seem relaxed. They often rest on the TV aerial and also perch to preen in a tall lime tree nearby.

They are primarily grain and small seed eaters but occasionally take elderberries in the early autumn.

For its nest site the collared dove usually chooses a conifer or other similar dense vegetation, or even apple trees if they are sufficiently tall and in a quiet situation.

If your garden is small, the chances of a pair settling down to nest are almost nil, especially if there is noise or continual movement by the occupants—but they will certainly call in for food.

The nest itself is an untidy affair, consisting of a rough platform of sticks, occasionally lined with grass roots, grassy stems and leaves, and sometimes hair is added. It is frequently built quite high—hence the need of well-established trees—anywhere where a branch joins the trunk and up to well over twelve metres above the ground.

The collared dove is increasingly regarded as a pest, chiefly because of its rapid increase, and the birds do occasionally go for newly emerged plants. Perhaps their constant visits to a liberal food source such as chicken runs, farmyards and even town and village streets makes them appear to be a nuisance. But they are attractive nevertheless, especially when they arrive at the bird table announced by their almost mechanical-sounding call.

I like them for they are quite handsome birds. Those that visit our bird tables almost invariably come in pairs, flying in together and perching close to each other. It seems obvious that they must pair for life, for the behaviour continues throughout summer and winter, except for occasional short spells, probably when one of them is incubating eggs.

During the winter months they thoroughly enjoy peanuts laid out on the table and in cold snowy weather swoop down to feed very soon after the nuts have been put out for them. They are non-aggressive to small birds which, in turn, seem unafraid of the collared doves.

DUNNOCK *(Prunella modularis)*. Hedge Sparrow, Shufflewing
An elegant, secretive bird, it spends much of its life skulking in hedgerows. The wilder the hedge, the better it likes it and far fewer are found in severely clipped hedges than where the farmer has allowed the bushes to sprout sideshoots. Thick, unkempt hedges are its favoured habitat and you will more often hear it than actually see it. It has a thin 'peep-peep' call, so quiet that it is almost un-birdlike, uttered secretively from the dark interior of the hedge.

Not only does the overgrowth provide shelter from wind, rain and cold nights, but there it finds all the food it needs. Grass seeds and many other small seeds fallen to the bare patches beneath the hedgerow bushes provide its basic diet.

Its wild habitats are recorded by Eric Simms in *Woodland Birds* as open woodland with undergrowth, groves, plantations, scrub, hedgerows, shrubberies and gardens, and in *Hedges* Pollard, Hooper and Moore describe it as a typical hedge species.

From the point of view of a bird gardener, plenty of bushy cover is indicated, and privet, escallonia, fuchsia and hawthorn hedges should encourage it to nest.

Its nest is a quite beautiful mossy cup, and despite its secretive placing is frequently parasitised by the cuckoo—a patient, observant and determined bird, although uncommon in most gardens.

The female does most of the nest-building but is accompanied by the male, and the nest is built as early as April; the pair often rear two broods, the second as late as August.

Most commonly, the nest is constructed almost entirely of moss—rough-stalked feather moss (*Brachythecium rutabulum*), long-trailing feather moss (*Eurhynchium praelongum*), and pale-trailing feather moss (*E. swartzii*)—with twisted grass stems and spiralled pieces of twig such as clematis leaf stalks. The rim is strengthened and smoothed by hair and, these days, by man-made fibres. Table 7, p. 93, gives details of nest sizes.

A recent nest I found demonstrated quite clearly how a bird will use any suitable nest material that is freely available, although in this instance the items were obviously not within the bird's normal experience. The nest was built in the hedge, close to a house which had a landing jetty on the estuary. The crabber who lived there had stacked some crab pots quite close by and, since these had been in use for some time, much of their net mesh-work was covered in sea fern (*Sertularia* spp). This must have proved irresistible to the dunnock, because she had gathered quantities of it and interlaced it with the mosses (these being the same species as those mentioned above). Being a true seafarer, this dunnock had also collected many strands of blue and red plastic rope threads from the ropework on the pots. Finally, and proving she collected material from her immediate neighbourhood, she had gathered innumerable fibres from an old coconut mat outside the back door, and with these she had made a wonderfully snug lining to the nest cup. It is interesting to note that all the materials used by her had been gathered within 18 metres of the nest site. A nautical, resourceful dunnock, if ever there was one.

As a bird garden bird it is high on the frequency list. Whilst written descriptions are widely open to the reader's personal interpretation, I shall risk it. To me it looks like a dainty sparrow (but much more timid) with a much more slender bill, and its body, although a warmish brown, appears quite pronouncedly striped with very dark stripes along the back from head into tail. Perhaps because it tends to 'stretch' forward close to the ground as it walks, it is easily recalled once it has been identified. Lest you should regard it as a dull bird, simply take a look at its beautiful nest and, with a minimum of disturbance, its wonderful blue eggs. And whilst it is called hedge *sparrow*, it is not a finch like the house sparrow but belongs to the same group as the robin and nightingale.

Its habit of wing-flicking has earned it the name of 'shufflewing' in some country districts.

GOLDFINCH *(Carduelis carduelis)*

How very fortunate we are that this delightful and colourful finch has adapted to living in places cultivated by humans. And whilst our hand has touched almost the whole of our land, the goldfinch shows a preference for nesting in parks and gardens in both suburban and country village areas. Although it does not feature as one of the top fifteen species in the BTO list of garden birds, many bird gardeners look forward each year to a visit.

It is an acrobatic little bird, whether clinging to the spiky heads of thistles, the stiff-thorned stem of teasel or the more mobile, swaying heads of knapweed and even ragwort. To cope with the massed prickles of many of its natural food plants the forehead and cheeks are equipped with rather stiffish hairs, to stand up to the constant buffeting they suffer.

Goldfinches' local movements are closely integrated with the seed times of their food plants, some of which are available throughout the year. It is during their food searching that they visit waste-ground—always a rich feeding ground for seed-eaters—and those other places where their food plants are growing.

A goldfinch nest is a most delicate structure of great beauty, composed of much very fine material. It is built by the female, most often accompanied by the male, and building takes place from late April; two broods may be reared between May and July and sometimes as late as August.

The base of the nest consists of a springy platform, mainly of very thin roots of grasses. All along the length of these twisty roots are small projections where side rootlets have broken off and it is these that bind together the entire base.

A few strands of moss, lichen and cupressus-like leaves are interwoven. One nest I saw had a large number of 75 mm long black bristles from a sweeping brush incorporated into the base.

The beautiful, soft round cup is usually lined with wool, hair of all kinds and plenty of the downy heads of dandelion and last year's thistle seeds. A few white feathers also form part of the cup wall.

Sometimes the rim is held together with the stems of Yorkshire fog, interspersed

with white cotton and white wool. Horsehair and hair from the tails of cattle, when obtainable, is twined several times around the rim.

The mosses used in the nests I have examined are: *Rhytidiadelphus squarrosus* which has stems up to 15 cm long and is at times a serious pest on lawns, *Hypnum cupressiforme* found on rocks, trees, walls, logs and on the soil too, and *Brachythecium rutabulum* which is common on trees, rocks and walls (see also p. 102).

Whilst there is obviously variation in nest size, most goldfinch nests come fairly close to the measurements given in Table 7 (p. 93).

The inside of the nest cup comfortably accommodates the body of the incubating bird which is a little less than 12 cm from bill to tail. In total the goldfinch's nest represents the ideal combination of lightness with strength, insulation, softness and springy firmness—a perfect home for growing nestlings.

GREAT TIT *(Parus major)*. Ox Eye, Sawfinch, Sawsharpener

In its wild habitat the great tit is a bird of broad-leaved, open deciduous woodland. Unlike the blue tit which feeds high in the trees, the great tit feeds low down and often on the ground itself. An under-storey of bushes and shrubs always proves an attraction in the wild and the same applies to our garden. For nesting, these birds favour large wooded gardens on the outskirts of towns, but that is not to say they will not take advantage of what is offered in a town garden—providing it is well supplied with shrubs. Certainly in the winter months they visit most gardens that provide a feeding place.

Great tits are very fond of beech nuts, but unfortunately the beech does not always produce a prolific harvest of nuts and this proves to be a bonus for those of us who have gardens in the vicinity of mixed woodland. Seeking alternative winter food, the tits may well come into our gardens for the peanuts we have to offer.

Caterpillars are sought in the summer oak woods and great tits usually go for some of the larger larvae. Again, as with the beech nuts, there are both abundant and scarce caterpillar years, and scarcity or plenty will have its effect on the breeding success of the birds and their young. Many people refer to these differing seasons as 'part of the balance of nature', but the term 'balance' usually implies equilibrium. Yet seldom is nature held in balance: always it is in a state of flux, with first one, then another species population rising or falling. In any prey-and-predator relationship there are peaks and depths—peaks as the prey species increases followed by a plunge as the predator species multiplies due to the abundant food supply. It is one factor which affects the ever-changing bird population of our gardens.

Opposite: *A wild corner of the garden with sowthistles and teasel crowded with seeds is an excellent way of encouraging goldfinches to come and feed. And what a pleasure it is to be able to watch these lovely birds feeding on plants that you grew especially for them. (Male below.)*

With its black cap, collar and throat and its white cheeks and yellow front divided by a black band, this bird is almost twice as large as any other British tit. In its natural deciduous woodland home, it frequents beech and hazel when they have shed their nuts, oak branches and limbs searching for insects, elder and hawthorn.

In general the great tit feeds on insects during the summer but searches for seeds in the winter, beech nuts, where available, forming much of its diet. It is quite strong enough to hold a hazelnut in its claws and smash it open with its powerful beak, a feeding action well beyond other tits.

Great tits are hole-nesters and take to nest boxes quite readily, but there is little doubt that the most favoured gardens are those with mature trees or else gardens in the vicinity of woodland, or even parkland which is well planted with trees.

A typical nest is made from moss and wool. A nest from a very rural situation had its base composed of layers of moss and the walls were thickly entwined with sheep's wool, which in places almost excluded the moss. No feathers were present. Whilst a nest is, at first glance, a delicate structure, it is amazing how strong it becomes as the bird twines the wool into the twisted, drying moss and binds the whole nest together.

From observing many nests made in nest boxes, it emerges that, like blue tits, great tits usually build the nest structure to fill the available floor space of the nest box, without altering the shape and size of the actual nest cup and its walls. It would seem the tits first build the nest itself and this is a light but inextricably interwoven structure mostly of hair, with wool and grass leaves. Having completed the 'normal' nest, quantities of moss with only a few grass leaves are added to fill in the spaces out to the wall, and this is very loosely packed—obviously no more than a fill-in job.

Some rural nests incorporate quantities of rabbit fur together with sheep's wool. Few feathers are used, usually less than a dozen, and in some nests feathers are absent.

The walls of the nest cup are lightly but most strongly built up with the materials interwoven, whilst the cup is softly lined with wool and hair.

It is wonderful that a nest can be so strong yet at the same time so light; with an average weight of 19g (moist as gathered), the weight of material carried is only a little more than the weight of the bird.

In a local oak wood, the great tits are quick to occupy nest boxes placed against the trunks of the oaks. In this particular wood the nest boxes were fixed from 2.5 to 3 metres above the ground level.

There is a strong feeling among many conservationists that, by placing large numbers of nest boxes in a wood, there is a tendency to increase the tit population well beyond its natural limits. This may then cause problems with predator-and-prey relationships and, indeed, impinge on the general distribution of other species. In a way, the same could be said of garden nest boxes, but research has also indicated that each site has a limit to its capacity which the birds do not exceed, even when additional boxes are available.

GREENFINCH *(Carduelis chloris)*. Greenchub, Green Linnet
A strikingly handsome finch when it flies off the singing perch, its bright yellow wing edges flashing in the summer sun. During winter feeding it resents the approach of other birds and will drive them off; even when food is abundant on the bird table it still ensures that other birds keep their distance.

Hence the value of having a large bird table so that there is less 'fighting' over the offered food, and consequently less disturbance for other species trying to feed at the same time.

Sometime during spring, usually in March, the male greenfinch perches on a tree limb and almost endlessly utters his song, and this he will continue to do until summer wanes. A few weeks later nest-building will begin, and despite its winter show of aggressiveness at the table, greenfinches often nest in colonies, perhaps five or six pairs spread over quite a small patch of suitable scrub or dense growth area in or near to hedges. To further confuse the issue, some pairs are solitary nesters.

The nest itself is a quite bulky structure of small thin twigs of dry weight 35 to 36 grams. One nest recently examined had 154 pieces of twig in its structure, a large proportion on the base being pieces of dead seed stems of dock with compacted grass, much of which was interwoven with rootlets. Unlike the neat nest of a chaffinch, the greenfinch's nest is very loosely constructed. Dry grass, moss and wool, when obtainable, form a warm cup. A variety of thin thread-like plant products are used to line the rim and the top of the soft cup. It is built by the hen, but much of the time the male accompanies her.

Winter is spent largely in flocks of mixed finches, feeding around farms and on cultivated ground. Essentially, this is a bird of the countryside and favours human activities only when they provide food in excess of what is found in nature. In winter, weed seeds such as spurrey, burdock, brassicas and cereals are eaten, and in spring diet changes to dandelion, ragwort and chickweed. After harvest it is back to cereals and the much favoured burdock (Ref. Newton, 1., 1967, *J. Anim. Ecol.* 36: 721–44).

All that was before the age of agrochemicals, and the abandonment of stackyards to the sacked grain of combine harvesters.

You may feel the farmyard and its land are remote from your bird garden, yet the open countryside provides so many clues to the way in which we can encourage birds to our own place.

Without any doubt, greenfinches prefer to approach a food source such as a bird table from the cover of a hedgerow, possibly because they move along such corridors looking for food. Having discovered your bird table they will return again and again until a change of season calls them to their breeding place.

Greenfinches are always attracted to peanuts in hanging dispensers and, unlike tits that will tolerate another clinging just above or below, the greenfinch likes to be alone. If you watch one feeding you will see that it spends much of its available feeding time looking out for possible new arrivals, or wing-flapping and threatening whenever another bird alights nearby. Count yourself fortunate if a pair choose to nest in your hedge, for it is much more likely to be a winter visitor/feeder.

Young great tits have a much duller plumage than their parents: their cap, instead of being jet black, is greyer, and they have yellowish cheeks. (Rose 'New Dawn' and Berberis rubrostila.)

HOUSE MARTIN *(Chelidon urbica)*

What a welcome sight is the arrival of this wonderful flier. Sometimes a few early migrants will be seen in March although the main body arrive during April. In flight it is easily recognisable by its bright white rump and forked tail. Those early birds so often encounter fierce and cold spring winds that keep the insects in cover, and after a long flight over land and sea they must be sorely in need of

House martin nest-building. It usually nests under eaves, inside roofs or sheds. It is with a sense of wonder that, later in the year, we may watch the fledglings depart on their long journey to South Africa, to return again the following year.

refuelling. To watch them fly over a neighbouring pond, dipping, rising and momentarily pausing to flutter and catch an insect, is to appreciate their intensely efficient eyesight. Imagine the problem: zipping through the air and sighting small flies at thirty yards' distance and adjusting flight path to coincide with the erratic movement of the prey insect. Quite staggering.

From April through to the middle of May the house martins will spend much of the day feeding in flight. Then comes the time for brief courtship, often on the ground with the female, wings a-quiver, inviting the singing male to mate. This sometimes occurs in the nest as well.

The nest is built by both sexes and once they have prospected the site under the eaves of a house, they work fast. Martins definitely prefer a good overhang, which after all offers better rain protection, and whilst sometimes a new nest position is decided upon, they often repair an old nest weathered from the previous year. Whichever is chosen, there is much work to be done. Their first task is to locate an area with soft wet mud, often beside a small stream or on the borders of a pond, then to pick up a pea-sized lump and carry it back and stick it onto the wall. Lump after lump is added, with some additional dried grass and the lining of fibres and soft straw and feathers (if available). The completed nest is shaped like half a basin and entry is through a small hole at the top. Four or five eggs are laid and each parent, turn by turn, incubates the eggs for about fourteen days.

An interesting aspect of house martin behaviour is the way in which the young of the first brood sometimes stay by the nest and help feed the nestlings of the second or even third brood.

If you are really keen to encourage house martins to nest on your house, why not fix two or three nest boxes under the eaves? (The design of such a box will be found in that excellent booklet BTO Guide 20 *Nestboxes*, by Chris du Feu, obtainable from the BTO). Even if the martins do not use them, their presence may encourage them to build natural nests nearby, because they are very social birds and often several will nest close together.

Quite the most fascinating fact about the young birds is that, at the age of twelve to sixteen weeks, they set off on a migration across continents including the Sahara desert, a journey of at least four to five thousand miles. We are only beginning to unravel the mystery of how it is accomplished. We know that scent and the earth's magnetic field, as well as their ability to take bearings from sun, moon and stars, are involved. Sometimes I find myself hoping that the mystery will never be solved. Surely, as humans, we need to know a few limits to our knowledge so that the sense of wonder is maintained. Scientists will tell you that the discovery of facts is an essential quest of humanity and that it inevitably leads to an increase in our sense of wonder. They are probably right, but as a simple bird lover I shall be content that each year they arrive and depart once more; to a romantic that mystery is far more intriguing than the understanding of too many facts. And it is always exciting when each spring the martins return, because *that is part of the real world.*

HOUSE SPARROW *(Passer domesticus)*

The sparrows' long sojourn around human habitation, its almost semi-domesticated tolerance of our presence and its ability to thrive on the rich variety of unconsidered trifles that result from our activities, has produced a little bird that is a great survivor. Like so many aspects of wildlife, the familiar is taken for granted. In the case of the sparrow, this tendency is a great loss to our pleasure in birds. As we shall see later, it is a fascinating little bird to watch, more especially because of its lack of timidity. A cock sparrow is definitely 'one of the boys'.

Many regard it as a nuisance. Admittedly it does cause some untidiness beneath its nest, and its inclination to share our roof space could be regarded as an annoyance. But for me the sound of a few sparrows twittering away at dawn just outside the bedroom window is a delight and arouses a sense of wonder that wild birds seeks to share our environment with us. It is one more proof that it is *we* who have striven to distance ourselves from wild creatures who, in the final analysis, are part of the same life force that envelops us all.

Unfortunately it is regarded as a pest on many farms where its love of grain conflicts with the farmers' economic interests. A flock of sparrows descending on a field of harvest-ready corn does cause minor damage, but in terms of total yield such a loss must surely be infinitesimal. Perhaps their fouling of stored grain when they make their way into barns is more serious, but even in these instances a little attention to bird-proofing and general repairs could settle the problem. So let us try and accept the sparrow on its own terms and enjoy its activities in our gardens.

Its nesting season extends from early April through to August and in warm years may even lengthen a month at each end. Favourite sites are in the eaves or in warm, sunny walls among thick growths of ivy, wistaria and clematis species. Basically it prefers to build its nest in a hole, but good dense cover seems to provide a pseudo-hole, where the very untidy nest is assembled. Both sexes build this nest and in the season you will see them flying to the site with all manner of material trailing from their beaks. If not built in a hole, the birds usually construct a domed nest, but sometimes they do not bother to do that and merely throw together a sort of heap of materials with a small depression in the middle. Quite frequently the new nest is built upon the dishevelled remains of a previous one, and somehow the untidy nest seems to reflect the life-style of most sparrows. They are a happy-go-lucky bunch, more fond of socialising than keeping a tidy house. I make no apologies for anthropromorphising because sparrows appeal to me on that level of relationship. I see so much of human attitudes in the sparrow's life-style that their behaviour provides food for thought.

The nest platform is laid upon the branches of the wall creeper and is really a mass of fibrous grass stems with intermingled moss. Next, a sort of improvised wall is built up and a very rough and ready rim is cobbled together to form a cup. Vast numbers of feathers are incorporated in the structure and this, to me, is an enigma. Where on earth do they find so many feathers? Look around your garden and you will be hard-pressed to find half a dozen, yet I have seen nests with nearly two hundred feathers in them. A representative number of nests contained 176, 179, 157, 123, 193 and 194 feathers—an average of approximately 170.

Bold and bustling, the house sparrow explores every inch of the garden, occasionally biting off a few petals—white is sometimes favoured—but mainly living off unconsidered trifles. The shy, retiring dunnock or hedge sparrow (left) is usually a lone individual who searches for seeds and small invertebrates in the cover of foliage.

One extraordinary nest, excluded from the average for obvious reasons, contained 387 feathers, 90 per cent of which were seagull feathers. This nest was close to a playing field where gulls roosted in the early spring and where much preening prior to sleep resulted in innumerable feathers being left in the grass. A short flight of 45 metres offered irresistible treasure trove to the ever-enterprising sparrows.

Another nest had quantities of tiny bright green and yellow feathers, obviously from a budgerigar. Indeed, some sparrows 'decorate' their nests—or maybe have simply been attracted to their finds—with all kinds of colourful material. I have found a Hamlet Cigar band, all shiny silver and gold, obviously collected by a bird that knew how to relax; pieces of fluorescent green paper, red plastic, pale green tissue paper and silver paper.

Generally the materials used reflect the type of 'rubbish' to be found around human habitation, such as grass, paper, binder twine, polythene strips, ivy leaves and stalks, straw, flowering heads of cocksfoot and Yorkshire fog, pieces of handkerchief tissue, kapok flocking, spiralled honeysuckle stem, wood shavings and glass wool. One nest had the cup lined with dogs' hairs and kapok.

A selection of mosses is used—rough-stalked feather moss, long-trailing feather moss, pale-trailing feather moss, and slender feather moss whose fruits in the spring with their bright red spore cases may possibly be a colour attraction to birds. An interesting feature of mosses is that they curl up as they dry, causing a multi-hook-like effect that helps to bind the nest together.

Five to six eggs are laid and incubated for around fourteen days and the nestlings are fed by both parents.

But fortunately there is so much more to enjoy with sparrows every day of the year.

At this very moment, on an August evening, there is a sparrow searching the grass within two metres of where I am sitting writing; two more have just flown into the wistaria amidst a great fluttering of wings, and by their twittering they are having a considerable difference of opinion over some aspect of their lives; another hen sparrow is clinging to the stems of a golden ash—again within a few feet of me—and she is examining the bark with exquisite care before hopping to the next and continuing the search. Even our springer, not always tolerant of birds at close quarters, lies stretched and relaxed as the busy sparrows come within a metre of her.

Some summer days, when you are relaxing on the lawn, the incessant chirping of a cock sparrow outside its nest under the eaves may slightly irritate by its repetition. At such times try to imagine how dull your garden would be if you did not share it with those little birds.

LONG-TAILED TIT *(Aegithalos caudatus)*. Bottle tit

This restless little bird usually arrives in gardens in early autumn and has the added attraction of coming in a party of six to eight. They wander acrobatically through the trees, always on the move except occasionally stopping for a morsel of insect food. All the while they give out their contact call of 'zi-zit, zi-zit', high-pitched and reedy, before flying to another bush to continue their exploration. As evening draws on they find a sheltered place and settle down close together. In fact this togetherness is typical of long-tailed tits and I have yet to see a solitary bird except of course at nesting time, when it is building or gathering food for nestlings.

Its nest is domed and highly elaborate, usually built in an inaccessible gorse bush or some other equally protected site. Felted moss forms most of the framework and both male and female build it together, weaving the mosses together with hair and spider's webs. The final outer covering is lichen and these pieces of many colours provide a thoroughly waterproof coating, at the same time making it a beautifully attractive nest—although that was not on the bird's list of priorities. The lining is the softest imaginable, being composed of literally hundreds of feathers, and Lewis Bonhote in his book *Birds of Britain*, published in 1907, states, 'as many as 700 feathers have been counted in a single nest'. Others have produced up to 2,000!

I have yet to see a long-tailed tit visit a bird table, which is not surprising since its diet is almost exclusively insectivorous. However, any garden that offers plenty of bushes and a tree or two will be going a long way to attracting a party during the winter months; provide a hedge with an occasional taller bush or tree in it and you will have provided an even better attraction.

If your garden is a rural one or else on the outer fringe of the suburbs you are more likely to be visited than in a town garden. It definitely favours 'green' country.

Its visit to your garden provides time to observe it with binoculars. Enjoy its active behaviour and beauty, for it may be many months before another party passes by.

PIED WAGTAIL *(Motacilla alba)*. Dishwasher

So frequently associated with water one almost expects to see it there, yet in fact it will be found in a variety of places including around buildings and farms. It will almost certainly be found near the local duckpond, walking through a shallow sheet of water left by a shower of rain. It is a bird that seems to enjoy the presence of man, and if I were an artist asked to draw one for identification purposes, I would paint it standing on a concrete path or area of tarmac beside a film of water. Although our garden is seldom visited, when it has flown in, it nearly always appears near the pond and on the lawn surrounding it. Whether or not that provides a clue to encouraging a pair into your garden remains to be proved, but a good lawn space always helps.

It is an active little bird with constantly bobbing tail flicking up and down—not sideways as the name suggests. It will walk a few paces, flit into the air calling its reedy song, alight, bob a lot and walk a little more, all the while pecking at mostly invisible insects on the ground. It seems to be in a constant fussy 'what do I do next?' frame of mind, never relaxed but all the more attractive for its ceaseless activity.

It feeds principally on insects of all kinds, and since water produces numbers of flies perhaps this is a reason for its attraction to water. It has a fondness for

Long-tailed tits preparing to roost in a Norway spruce. Only an infrequent visitor to the garden when, perhaps as a family party, they are en route to a fresh feeding site. These fascinating little birds roost close together so that the shared warmth of their tiny bodies helps them to survive cold frosty nights. But night is their enemy, and sometimes even their huddled closeness cannot withstand the penetrating weather.

bathing and one of its Victorian names was Polly Dishwasher or just Dishwasher.

The favourite nesting place is a hole in a wall or cavity behind ivy, built by the female although the male accompanies her. The base of the nest consists of a few solid twiggy and knobbly growths whilst the body is built up with sheep's wool, dog's hair and similar fibres intertwined with meshed grass stems. A few pieces of twisty rootlets of grass or other plants are incorporated and together these items make a light, strong and springy nest. A large quantity of moss is interwoven, including species such as *Hypnum mammillatum* and oak moss (*Eurhynchium praelongum*). Occasionally, pieces of a greyish-green lichen such as *Evernia prunastri* are used.

Within the cup so formed is a warm lining of downy seeds with thistledown and groundsel and a few feathers added. A few unusual substances are sometimes collected, among which may be found coloured plastic thread, knitting wool and thin shreds of string. The entire nest is a neat structure with a cup of around 7 cm enclosed by a cup rim of about 3 cm thickness. The cup itself may be 5 cm or more deep.

Unusual nest sites are often chosen. I have seen a nest built in a hanging basket in a school where hundreds of children passed noisily to and fro daily. Perhaps the most unusual thing about it was that every day the basket was very thoroughly watered, and whilst the nest rested among some lobelia, a close-by geranium hardly shed the water. An even more surprising site was reported in the *Western Morning News*. A pair of pied wagtails used the Suzuki jeep of a restaurant owner and built their nest on the engine to rear a family, despite the man driving around Devon. Amidst the noise of the motor, whirring fan belt and fan the pair successfully reared the five young. Since wagtails frequently return to a nest site, it will be interesting to see what happens next spring.

ROBIN *(Erithacus rubecula)*. Robin Redbreast

Sentimentalised, anthropromorphised in children's books, and highly commercialised in wrapping paper and greeting cards, this attractive little bird has become the bird image of Christmas. It is indeed Britain's national bird. Extremely secretive in late summer when it undergoes moult, at other times of the year it will join the gardener and collect worms within a foot of the working spade.

In its natural habitat it is a bird of the undergrowth in deciduous and coniferous woodland, and anyone who has walked a woodland path will be aware of the beady-eyed redbreast taking a good look from a bramble stem or vantage point of a low bush. Pause in your walk and it flutters away, keep moving and it will occasionally let you come quite close before moving ahead once more.

On the ground and in the sheltering shade of low-growing shrubs it finds all it wants to eat. It will stand motionless, its sharp eyes watching for the slightest movement before alighting to seize a small beetle creeping from the cover of a leaf, a centipede crawling under a rotting twig, an ant or perhaps a worm disturbed earlier by a leaf-scrabbling blackbird. Its habit of so frequently feeding in cover ensures a steady supply of available food, for in inclement weather, flies and all kinds of small insects also seek shelter in such places.

Whilst robins will often join other birds mobbing a predator, I recently experienced an instance of how familiarity with a predator alters behaviour. A pair of robins had nested in the hole of a hedgerow oak, within a few yards of the nest hole of a pair of tawny owls in another nearby tree. It was late June and the owls were busy collecting food for their hungry owlets. For several days in succession, an hour before dusk, I went into the hide and waited. Every time without fail, about half an hour later, the cock robin would fly to the same branch and start a quiet scolding—a sure sign that the owl had appeared. Yet that robin never became really assertive as mobbing birds become and I feel sure it was because the little bird had come to realise that the owls represented no threat to itself.

It is not surprising that such an attractive and interesting little bird has been the subject of much scientific study, and anyone who wishes to become intimately acquainted with the life-style of the redbreast should read David Lack's classic, *The Life of the Robin*, a truly wonderful in-depth study packed with many fascinating facts. His other book on this subject, *Robin Redbreast*, is also a wonderfully informative read. Chris Mead's *Robins* is full of enjoyable knowledge on its life. Indeed, so many scientific papers have been published on its habits that it can no longer claim to have a private life of its own!

The nest is built by the female, all the material being gathered and carried to the nest site within a very few days, usually at the beginning of April. The site shows great adaptability and the selected items are legion. Indeed, I remember vividly my first encounter with a robin's nest when I saw the bird fly out from a builder's site hut that had a broken door. A brief search quickly revealed the nest, cosily built within the gaping pocket of an old coat hanging in the corner. And each spring the newspapers report unusual nests ranging from old tins, thrown-away household utensils and unexpected receptacles in garden sheds and huts. All these are so different from their sites in the wild woods that one wonders why they select them. However, all have the common property of offering a well-protected dry cavity. And that is what a robin seeks—holes in a hedgebank, a small ledged cavity beneath an overhanging bank beside a woodland path, broken trees and the shelter of plant growth around tree trunks. But all must offer dense cover, for in its nest site selection the little bird is most secretive.

A nest site in a garden may well be situated amongst a thick growth of ivy growing up a house wall, or in the angle between a garage and the house, like a nest I found. Materials used in this nest consisted of a base of dead leaves of many kinds, built into the ivy stems. These were interspersed with pieces of moss—rough-stalked feather moss and pale-trailing feather moss—very small clumps of grass such as gardeners remove when weeding, and many grass stems which were loosely entwined with the moss together with a few skeletonised hydrangea petals—it is surprising in how many nests of garden birds these appear. This was built up to form a cup approximately 7 cm inside diameter. One or two 38 cm long hairs were twined in and were possibly horse or cattle hair, but the inside of the cup was snugly lined with 251 dogs' hairs. I am not proposing that these were collected one at a time, but nevertheless they must have been searched for and gathered with considerable selective care. The robin's beady little eyes certainly picked them out from all the varied 'rubbish' that accumulates beneath bushes. Again it is worth nothing that the rootlets used, most up to 15 cm in length, were less than .25 mm in diameter, very contorted and probably from couch grass.

The nest weighed only 75g, but bear in mind this was all carried by a small bird weighing 19 to 20g. The entire nest could be described as well fashioned, tidy but not especially neat, although the walls of the cup, which were about 3 cm thick, were quite regular in thickness.

Due to its quiet secretive nature, a robin may well occupy a nest site in your patch without your being aware of its presence. But sit quietly and watch, and more will be revealed than you could possibly have imagined.

And how long does a robin live? Well averages, in the matter of life and death, seem rather out of place, but a long-lived bird may be around your garden for eight years, although many fledglings and young die in the first two years of life. Perhaps the main cause of death is poor feeding in harsh winters, for a small bird needs a constant supply of energy-giving food, every day. Being a species given to 'trusting' humans, the robin is often too casual in its manner of feeding. This renders it easy prey to a patient cat, and many die in this way.

Whilst the cock robin in your garden may live there throughout its life, and within a few metres of the nest in which it was born, a number of females do tend to move around. Some robins even migrate abroad, but these are but a very small minority of the resident population.

So enjoy your resident robin, and whilst appreciating its apparent 'tameness', realise that it is a *wild bird*, which has come to accept you and your garden as food providers. It is simply supplying a basic survival need. But are we not fortunate that such a delightful little bird satisfies that need in our own garden?

SONG THRUSH *(Turdus philomelus)*. Throstle, Mavis
The song thrush is an elegant, shy, very selective feeder and a bird of somewhat retiring manner, acutely alert in the presence of humans. Despite its popularity as a songster it is not as common in gardens as one might imagine. The BTO survey of the top fifteen species occurring in gardens during the summer of 1988 showed it halfway down the list in suburban gardens at 44 per cent, slightly higher in rural gardens at 53 per cent. During a winter survey it did not appear in the top twelve list at all. There seems to be a quite definite tendency towards a decline in the numbers of song thrushes, and expert opinion offers few answers as to why this should be so.

However, during the past two decades, the massive increase in the use of fungicides, insecticides, and herbicides, coupled with slug pellets, hormone sprays and other chemical weapons, may well have contributed to this loss simply by killing off much of the food supply or by contaminating the food and causing a build-up of lethal toxins within the birds' bodies. The general change in agricultural methods such as spraying, removal of hedges, ploughing up of permanent grassland and drainage of wetland places would also seem to contribute to a deterioration of the habitats that provide home and shelter for such creatures as snails.

Wherever one goes these days chemicals are at work as local authorities spray

Although the robin's natural nest site is usually in the hollow of a bank, among thick foliage or a tree-hole, it sometimes chooses man-made and discarded articles. But *always* the nest is thoroughly concealed. So, if you decide to put out an old kettle, hide it in foliage—much better to try an open-fronted nest box.

verges, park flowerbeds, grassed areas, kerbs, pavements and pathways. Many of
these places again provide habitat for snails and worms, and one can hardly
imagine such substances enhancing the environment of the thrush's food species.
It seems possible that the great increase in domestic pets, with their consequent
disturbance factor, may also make a contribution to the decline.

Maybe it is so, maybe no. But for certain, fewer song thrushes are now seen in
gardens.

In habitats where they survive, their favourite food is the dark-lipped banded
snail (*Cepaea nemoralis*), and the white-lipped banded snail (*Cepaea hortensis*),
both of which the thrush hunts by sight. The latter snail is extremely variable in
colour patterns, from thick black bands to thin ones, completely yellow and
completely pink shells.

It is interesting to reflect that the thrush's predation on this snail has had some
effect on the colour patterns evolved. Those patterns more easily spotted by the
bird will be eaten whereas the better camouflaged ones will survive. If you examine
the shell particles around any thrush's anvil you will see more banded snails than
the common garden snail. In the wild woodland, hedge bottoms and grassland the
dark-lipped snail is more preyed upon because those are its natural habitat,
whereas whilst the white-lipped does occur in similar habitats, it is much commoner
in a damper and cooler habitat. In gardens the common garden snail is more
commonly eaten, chiefly because it is more abundant.

The favourite anvil is a stone, and one sure way of knowing that a thrush is
nearby is when you discover the mass of broken snail shells around a stone. The
bird will also use wood as a breaking surface, and I recall a small wooden bridge
over a drainage ditch in the fens that had literally dozens of broken banded snail-
shells spread all over it. In that marshy, soft ground there were no stones but
plenty of snails, so the thrush used the next most convenient material.

An alternative food, certainly for those thrushes within reasonable distance of
the sea, is provided by marine univalves. Especially when frost and snow covers
the land snails, thrushes go to quiet rocky shores where they feed on periwinkles
and no doubt other sea molluscs. It is a natural extension of their feeding environment and a plentiful food source, for even in the hardest winter weather a rising
tide removes the effects of frost and seashore univalves are always on the move.

Song thrushes also feed on worms and on lawns they can be watched as they
stand motionless with head cocked to one side, obviously listening for movement
in a worm hole.

In choosing a nesting site this bird invariably seeks dense, deep foliage such as
might be found in conifers, thick foliaged hedgerows, hollies and hawthorns and
often creepers against walls, providing they have not been too closely pruned and
have an abundance of leaves—another indication of its retiring habit.

The female does the building, beginning in late March, and the nest season may
extend as late as August. She gathers many kinds of thin woody, springy stems,
usually about 10–13 cm in length, such as the rhizomes of couch grss, stems of
forsythia prunings and pieces of soft, rotten wood. Ivy stems and others are
collected when damp and used to build up the walls of the nest; ivy in particular,

when available, is favoured. Since much nest-building is carried out during the early part of the morning, the various materials collected will be damp from early season dew or are often collected from shady damp areas where such materials always seem to be.

Providing there is plenty of rain to moisten the soil, she then sets about bringing in beakfuls of mud which are pushed into the grass stems and roots to form a sort of wattle and daub foundation for the neat and precise plastering job to follow. The mud is well mixed with soft and malleable wood fragments to produce a mortar-like mixture which the bird has quite obviously selected for its consistency. She now begins to shape the cup by turning her body round and round, all the while pressing her breast against the walls to a 3–4 mm thickness. In a well-constructed nest the beautiful symmetry and smoothness of the inside of the cup is a wonder to be seen, and as it dries so it increases in strength. The top part of the cup is usually composed of a semi-woven wall of grass stems, and a few small rootlets and occasional thin twigs, the entire structure firmed in place with mud, some of which is plastered over the top of the rim.

Some nests have this basal platform composed of additional items such as clumps of grass stems, cerastium and aubrieta stems with their dried and twisty leaves still in place, cupressus leaves (a favoured item with many garden nesters) and skeletonised leaves and the dried skeletonised petals of hydrangea.

The total dry weight of a thrush's nest may range between 90 and 125g. Bearing in mind that most of the material will be gathered when moist, its damp weight will be in the neighbourhood of 300g. So, since the body weight of a thrush may average around 85–90g, the bird carries about four times its own weight to make its nest—a very considerable expenditure of energy, which also underlines its need for a staple diet, freely available.

The general dimensions of the nest will be found in Table 7, p. 93.

Despite the technical details of nest-building the greatest pleasure to be shared with the thrush is its musical, pure song, whether mingling with the dawn chorus or pleasured from its singing post, hopefully in a tree in your garden. A truly elegant and delightful bird.

For fuller information on the foods taken by song thrush and other members of the thrush family there is an excellent summary by P.H.T. Hartley in *British Birds*, 47, pp. 97–107, 'Wild Fruits in the Diet of British Thrushes'. As with most scientific papers, it is possible to obtain photocopies from the libraries of the bird societies, from the British Museum (Natural History), or from the publication itself.

STARLING *(Sturnus vulgaris)*
In our garden it is a case of 'where do all the starlings go in the summertime?' for there is always a spell between April and August when very few of them come to visit us. Nevertheless, there are days when they arrive in parties of adults which are quite obviously introducing their young to good food situations. At such times the grey-brown youngsters stay very close to their parents, almost in the shadow of their bodies! Their arrival is spectacular. The gathering descends amidst a flurry

of wings and endless starling chatter, for they are noisy, garrulous birds and their offspring no less so.

There is a pear tree overlooking our garden; for one reason or another the fruit is never gathered in and each year—according to the ripening season—the starlings arrive to peck away at the fruit. But they never come until the week it is fully ripe. The wasps follow in to sup the sugary juice exposed and down among the grass on the fallen yellowing fruit, full of starling peck-marks, tortoiseshell, red admiral and peacock butterflies stretch out their tongues and feed. Quite a wildlife bonus, simply because the fruit was left for the birds.

Each year one pair nests in our roof, entering through a small hole. Indeed humans, with their buildings and habitations, have provided very attractive habitats for starlings, hence their nesting near our gardens.

In the nearby deciduous wood a number of starlings nest in the hollow trees that a beneficent management permits to remain. Invariably they choose a hole formed where a branch has broken away from the trunk and which has rotted out. In some years starling, apart from those nesting there, come to the wood and feast on the tortrix caterpillar plague. In the same way that word is spread when food is put out in the garden, the message draws the birds into the woodland.

Are such messages connected with song? To what extent do birds sing for pleasure? Starlings are one of the few species that 'sing' throughout the year and many a winter afternoon is lightened by a group of them perched on our TV aerial. For a half-hour or more, as they wait for the main roosting flock to arrive, they chatter away to each other. Personally I am convinced this is a way of communicating to each other, and who is to say a starling cannot tell of its feeding activities? There's more to a starling than is ever dreamed of! For instance, listen to them and you will hear woodland and bird calls of buzzard and green woodpecker, or maybe the mimic will render a distant curlew—all calls that prove the bird has visited their habitats and learned those calls.

Starling enjoy feeding on a moist or wet lawn where they push their opened beaks to pick up worms, leather jackets and any other small invertebrates that may be lingering in the cool shade. Such feeding on lawns is merely an extension of their habit of feeding in farm grassland. And the spiders they consume must be truly astonishing. W.S. Bristowe, in his book *The World of Spiders*, records that in a Sussex field which had remained undisturbed for a considerable time, he found more than two million spiders to the acre. That represents a pretty hefty feast for a flock of starlings. Even today, when one year leys have superseded the old long-term meadows, the spider population must still provide a considerable part of the bird's diet.

From the viewpoint of the bird gardener starlings present a problem, for in the winter their numbers are supplemented by countless arrivals from the continent. Russia, the Baltic States, Poland, Germany, Sweden, Norway, Finland, Denmark and the Low Countries—each contributes to the arrivals at your bird table. Whether you wish to encourage or discourage them in your garden will depend on what you wish to achieve, but an idea for a 'starling preventer' is included in the chapter on feeding (p. 68).

By choice, the bird is a hole-nester, and in the wild a hollow tree with a small entrance hole is a favourite site; in the garden environment, however, it may find a space under the eaves, in an unused chimney (a frequent cause of blockage when fires are lit in the winter), or in a nest box. Apparently in the past they often nested in haystacks, but such nest sites are no longer available as such stacks are now exceedingly rare.

The nest is an untidy affair composed of grass, hay or straw and with a rough lining of feathers.

The starling is a bird that positively enjoys bathing and so will be a frequent visitor to the bird bath where it thoroughly soaks itself as it scatters drops far and wide amid much wing-shuffling and body-shaking. This is quite typical of the bird — untidy and hyperactive in everything it does.

A sight never to be forgotten is the arrival of a roosting flock of starlings. Their roost may be in a group of tall trees, on the ledges of a city building or, like the one I know, in a reed bed. Imagine with me the evening scene. The sun has already set, but the sky still holds a hint of blue and towards the horizon a drift of dark smoke appears. Yet no smoke ever moved like that, swinging from side to side, swirling first down and then upwards and ever growing larger. Very quickly the haze resolves itself into specks, the specks into individual birds and then with the roar as of a sudden gale of wind the starlings sweep overhead. The beat of their wings numbs the senses; their numbers, uncountable, stagger the mind. Lower they come and lower until the shadowed horde sweeps across the reed beds and sets the stems quivering and swaying. Two or three more swirls of breathtaking aerobatics weaving against the darkening sky and they alight. Quite suddenly each golden reed is blackened with the still bodies of birds. Still but not silent. For a great chattering now fills the lake and then another massed take-off, more circling, followed by a settling into the roost. The reeds bend over with their burden of birds, the bird calls suddenly cease and then in their thousands they fall asleep. Here and there a few birds flutter to secure a better toe-hold, but within minutes silence returns. Three-quarters of a million starlings have settled down for their night's sleep!

SWALLOW *(Hirundo rustica)*

As it flies northwards with the coming of spring, one wonders where this bird roosts. Before leaving South Africa, large bands of European swallows roosted in reed beds. There, with no feeding duties to contend with, they spent much of the day alone or perhaps a few together. Then, as dusk set in, they assembled, and some very remarkable numbers have been counted — well into hundreds of thousands. Does it fly high in the night sky, remaining on the wing? How does it sleep? Up to the present we do not know, but although 'two swallows do not a summer make', we know with certainty that with the coming of spring they will be with us. By May they will be cutting through the air above open country, tail-streamers and red forehead, face and throat making them easy to identify.

Whilst house martins always nest on the outside of buildings, swallows invariably nest *inside*. Such buildings as open sheds, barns, and old buildings are favoured as nest sites. One season I was privileged to spend several weeks watching the entire process of their domestic life as we sat in a hide within three metres of the beam on which the nest was built.

The feeding of the nestlings occupied the parents most of the day. Sitting in the half-light of the shed, we would see a sudden flash of wings and four beaks would snap open as the parent flew towards the gaping yellow mouth. Such was the urgency of feeding that the adult simply hovered against the nest as the beakful of insects was thrust down an ever-hungry nestling, before flying off once more to trawl through the air and catch more flies. A pause of half a minute and the other adult would arrive. Then another pause, perhaps a minute or two minutes, and the first parent would return again.

It was one of those summers when sunny weather gave way to misty rain, and that really caused problems. In fact, had not the weather changed after a week, the youngsters must surely have died. Even swallows cannot catch enough flies for four hungry nestlings when the air is cold and wet. At an age of about sixteen days the youngsters were amply filling the nest and the feeding frenzy rose to a new crescendo. Flies may be rich in protein but they are small in bulk, and it seemed those chicks reacted to bulk more than the finer details of the diet. On about the twenty-sixth day, towards the end of June, the youngsters flew the nest, and for the ensuing eight weeks they appeared from time to time, feeding and flying overhead.

We did not see them depart, but one day the sky was no longer criss-crossed by their aeronautics and in a small way my heart went with them as they travelled south with another rising spring in the Union of South Africa. Fortunate birds to live in perpetual spring and summer.

Any time you have an evening to spare among the birds, go to a nearby pond, lake or reservoir; there you will find the swallows flying and feeding. If you observe very closely you will see one sweep down and skim the water surface as it drinks on the wing. Simply watching their aerial manoeuvres with those skilful twists, glides, banking and sudden turns is to begin to appreciate their mastery of flight. Yes, it is natural to them, instinct and learning both involved, yet there *is* something very special about a bird's flight.

There is little you can do to attract swallows to your garden, but you can most certainly enjoy them as they fly over your garden and if it is a rural one you *may* be fortunate enough to have a nesting pair.

WREN *(Troglodytes troglodytes).* Stumpy, Jenny Wren
Tiny, but a great character, this little bird is highly successful and one of our most widespread. The male, in the breeding season, builds several nests in its selected territory, but completes none of them until its mate shows a preference for a particular one. Feathers are then collected by the female to form a warm lining. If the situation is a little exposed, a dome is built onto the nest.

The actual site is extremely varied, but very popular are large cracks, crannies and crevices in mossy banks, often near the top where vegetation spills over and provides shelter. Fallen trees offer sites among the twisted roots as do piles of sticks, drifts of dead bracken and, more often than not, another bird's nest. On one occasion a wren lined a swallow's nest in a barn, laid six eggs and incubated whilst some swallows in a nearby nest were struggling to feed their young. It was one of those misty, wet summers with rain day after day, and the swallows found few insects in flight. The result was that one of the parents and two young died from exhaustion. In the meantime the wrens prospered. Their success was undoubtedly due to their habit of finding food in dense hedgerows—the insects had gone to ground and the wrens found butterflies, moths, harvestmen, flies and other insects in abundance. Six little wrens flew the nest. Fortunately also, the lone swallow reared two young, but only after a tough struggle to find food.

An unusual site recently reported in the press was in one of the pockets of a pair of denim jeans. Five eggs were laid whilst the jeans were hanging on the washing line!

The nest illustrated overleaf was built in an open-fronted outhouse where a coil of nylon rope was hanging from a beam. It was an extremely firm structure, 140 mm from top to bottom and 110 mm wide, with a tiny 25 mm entrance hole near the top. The structure was made of leaves with entwined grass stems; the former had obviously been collected when damp because they had set into twisted shapes which actually added strength; poplar, ivy and elm were used and a quantity of moss incorporated on the outside. Skeletonised leaves were plentiful. The entrance hole was made firm by being surrounded by inter-twined grass stems with moss pressed firmly into it. The whole effect was of a smooth and well-rounded entrance.

The following details show the proportions of materials used.

Dry weights		*Percentage*
Leaves	21.7 g	38.3
Moss*	24.8 g	43.8
Small twigs and grass	7.5 g	13.3
Total dry weight of nest	56 g	

Some idea of the amount of work involved in building this nest can be gauged from the fact that over a period of many days the tiny bird had carried materials which totalled several times its own body weight. Multiply that by the four or five extra nests made by the male and you can see that nest-building for the wren involves considerable effort.

Wrens struggle for survival in a cold, wet winter; a small bird needs a constant food supply and they have few reserves of energy-giving fat. You may well observe wrens coming to your bird table towards the end of the year and perhaps into late December, after which their numbers decline—alas, too frequently from dying of exposure or hunger. More than 60 per cent of our population of wrens died in the cold winter of 1962–63, yet today there may be more than ten million of them thriving once more.

Happily, with two broods of four to seven eggs, incubated for a fortnight by the female, and the fledglings all fed on summer plenty—mostly by a busy female

* See p. 102 for moss species used.

and only occasionally by the male—the young will leave the nest and fly free after some 18 days. Certainly, if the male was busy constructing the nests, the female more than does her share later on, often rearing two broods between April and July. For such a tiny bird that represents a very considerable expenditure of energy and it must work very hard seeking the insects and small invertebrates needed to stoke up on. But wrens are highly skilled in searching the cover of bushes where such small forms of life are sheltering and only in the coldest of wet winters do they succumb.

As befits the tiniest bird that once graced our farthing, formerly our smallest coin, the Jenny Wren enhances any garden. But despite its pert and cocky appearance with upthrust tail, it is a retiring little bird, much more appreciative of good shaded cover than the bright open spaces among the flowers.

Recent BTO surveys show that wrens seem to prefer rural gardens, but recent years have shown an increased use of both rural and urban gardens. It is also possible that the recent succession of mild winters followed by hot summers has helped to maintain their population numbers.

Quite recently we were driving along a lane beside a stream, between high hedgebanks and over-arching trees. It was rather like a long tunnel and what astonished us was the number of wrens that flew from one hedge to the other just in front of the car. In less than half a mile we counted eighteen. It was early spring and those wrens had certainly survived the mild winter; no doubt that shady lane with its ample hedgerow cover provided just what the little birds needed. Perhaps most importantly, very little traffic used the lane as was evidenced by the strip of grass growing down its centre.

It seems there is very little we can do actually to encourage a wren to settle down, and any success we may have is not always attributable to our garden planting, but rather to the nature of the surrounding environment. Certainly we will be more fortunate in a rural environment or in a garden that has become overgrown. But once it has settled in you may well hear its shrill call around Christmas-time, and throughout the year, occasionally at night. Whilst usually solitary when not in the breeding season, wrens sometimes gather together to roost on a cold winter's night and at such times they may even use nest boxes. Like so many intriguing aspects of bird life, one wonders what it is that arouses normally solitary birds, living a little distance apart, to gather into a tiny space to spend the night. But that mystery is part of the magic that keeps alive our sense of wonder.

A coiled rope was left in a garden shed, and this wren nested there for two years. Male wrens build several nests before the female finally decides which is most suitable for the family. She then constructs a soft lining within, before laying her eggs.

WINTER VISITORS

Depending on where you live in the British Isles, but usually after a few days of intense cold accompanied by heavy snowfall, your garden may well be visited by fieldfare and redwing. Their home range on the moors has been covered by snow and their food locked away in a natural deep freeze. So down to the lowlands they fly and, especially if you are near the sea where the ocean so often keeps the land a little warmer, they find food and relief.

Now is the time for you to place a few apples out on the ground (providing it is reasonably cat-free), or on a large table in the middle of your snow-covered lawn. Both fieldfare and redwing are berry feeders and both have almost certainly been enjoying the rowan berries and sloes on the moors.

FIELDFARE (*Turdus pilaris*). Blueback, Feet, Felt, Felfer
This member of the thrush family has a much more restricted diet than the blackbird, song thrush, mistle thrush and ring ousel, and when hard weather sends the birds to our gardens, they seem to prefer to search in the undergrowth beneath trees and bushes, where fallen leaves hide worms, beetles and spiders. From October until March their diet comprises earthworms and molluscs in about equal quantities, with fruit and berries as available, and invertebrates in late winter and spring.

Due to their life habits there appears to be little we can do to encourage them into our gardens, but nevertheless if we have a few berry-bearing shrubs such as hawthorn, holly, crab apple, guelder rose, rowan and pyracantha, they may feed on these in times of snow and intense cold.

The season to look out for fieldfares extends from their migration arrival in September to their departure in March, and a few may even remain into April. Seldom do they arrive singly, for they are a species that tends to feed in flocks and locally such flocks number from twenty to thirty individuals.

They are handsome birds, very upright and alert, but very wary of human kind. Perhaps this is largely due to their spending much of the year on wild moors and quiet farmland where they encounter people only occasionally. Fieldfares seldom allow you to approach closer than a hundred feet, except in freezing conditions when the search for food overcomes their fear. Keep still and watch quietly and you will be rewarded by their visit.

REDWING (*Turdus iliacus*). Swinepiper, Wind Thrush
Often seen in company with flocks of fieldfare, the smaller redwing is immediately recognised by the pale eye stripe and reddish plumage along the flanks. This bird is very subject to the effects of hard weather, chiefly because of hunger. It will then change its normal diet of invertebrates and worms to berries such as yew, ivy and holly. But in some hard years such berries have already been stripped by other birds that tend to feed on berries rather than invertebrates. Many a redwing may well have been saved by the fact that the ivy has berries all winter, although they do not ripen until late spring.

Long before you see one in your garden you may hear them. On a quiet, dark night in October, if you are fortunate enough to be on their arrival route you will hear their faint whistling call high in the night sky.

One winter I saw dozens of redwings rooting among the snow-covered autumn leaves on a woodland road. They barely moved far enough to allow the car to pass by. The interesting aspect of this encounter was the fact that a blizzard had hit the moors only twenty-four hours before and the birds had immediately come down to the coast—a highly efficient survival strategy.

SISKIN (*Carduelis spinus*)

It is always an exciting moment when one of these little birds alights on the peanut dispenser, for they are infrequent visitors to many gardens, especially in the south. For some reason that has yet to be explained, siskins are particularly attracted to those red, nylon-mesh bags commonly used to dispense peanuts—to such an extent that the bags have become known as siskin bags. From Scandinavia they migrate south, especially in those years when the birch seeds, which are so important in their diet, are scarcer than usual. Their arrival dates vary from late in September through October and in some years November, and they stay until April.

The siskin is a bird of the coniferous woodlands, especially spruce, and in autumn and winter when the birch seeds and alder cones are plentiful it moves to areas where they grow. But it is often late winter into early spring before it comes to visit many of us.

Because of its preference for conifers it has begun to show a spread into gardens. According to the BTO *Population Trends in British Breeding Birds* by John H. Marchant, Robert Hudson, Steve P. Carter and Phil Whittington: 'Wintering siskins have been able to take advantage of ornamental conifers planted in parks and gardens. Perhaps as a consequence of being attracted to gardens in that manner, they have more recently taken to feeding on supplementary foods, especially peanuts.'

This is another striking example of a bird species being very habitat-conscious, and plainly demonstrates how we, as gardeners, may be able to encourage siskins into ours by planting conifers. Creating habitat is always the key to open the garden gate to birds of all species.

In behaviour the siskin is almost tit-like, exhibiting much the same gymnastic skills as it twists, turns and uses its feet to seize and grip unlikely footholds.

Perhaps due to its liking for coniferous woodland, it is more of a rural bird than a town visitor, although suburban gardens may be more fortunate. It is an attractive bird with its yellow-green plumage and black crown that give a flash of bright colour as it flies to and fro in the garden.

Persist with your red peanut bags and possibly a suet container, and keep a sharp look-out during the winter months. This may be your lucky year.

Redwing (left) *and fieldfare* (right) *will feed on apples when snow covers the ground. By storing a few of your summer crop you may help those birds to survive when little else is available. Place the fruit out on the lawn or compost heap but keep a watch out for the local cat.*

OCCASIONAL VISITORS

GOLDCREST (*Regulus regulus*)

Great excitement when one of these flies into your garden—in ours only two have been seen in the past ten years, and then only for a brief passing-by. If you happen to live near a fir or conifer woodland, or even a deciduous wood well planted with conifers, you stand a slightly better chance of enjoying this active, restless little bird.

As an eater of insects and spiders, the goldcrest is easily affected by very cold winters. At such times the scarcity of food and intensely cold night temperatures cause a sudden drop in its numbers in its natural habitat, and consequently in gardens.

Perhaps, rather like the siskin, the goldcrest has shown an initial preference for gardens with conifers or firs, but your chances of actually attracting any by planting such trees is extremely remote. However, we should never forget that garden conifers do enrich and increase the diversity of habitat, even in the smallest of gardens.

GREAT SPOTTED WOODPECKER (*Dendrocopus major*). Pied Woodpecker

This woodpecker may turn up in quite unexpected places. One regularly visits a nearby suburban garden and actually came in to feed there only a few days after the owners moved in and put the nuts out—yet nearby gardens were seldom visited. A feature of this garden is its large trees, including an aged apple tree, so maybe the aspect of habitat recognition is involved here. The best you can do is put out some nuts, preferably hanging from a tree, and wait and see. It would be a useful research project to investigate the tree composition of gardens visited by such species and to record the garden's situation with regard to the surrounding environment. Such investigatory work could be carried out on one or two of the locally resident species, which only occasionally come into gardens.

GREEN WOODPECKER (*Picus viridis*). Yaffle
The Yaffle with its wild ringing call is basically an insect eater, but it is fond of visiting gardens with ant-infested lawns and it is there you are most likely to see one. It is a bird with an extremely long tongue which it extends down into ant galleries and the boring tunnels of tree-boring beetles. As far as I am aware, there is very little you can do to attract it. Quite simply you are lucky if you get an occasional visit.

A regular visitor to some gardens, the green woodpecker eats enormous numbers of ants either on the lawn or in the flowerbeds or fruit plot. Its loud, laughing cry is a wonderful sound, almost unique in the bird world.

JACKDAW (*Corvus monedula*). Jackdaw Kae, Chough, Cadder or Caddy, Cathedral Parson, Jaypie, Devil Scritch, Oak Jackdaw, Scold, Keeper's Friend, Keeper's Watchdog

An occasional visitor to the table and a handsome bird, too. For a wonderful description of the jackdaw's behaviour you should read *King Solomon's Ring* by Konrad Lorenz. It is an amazing story of how Lorenz came to know them and, what is even more surprising, how the birds came to know him. We reared a rejected nestling one year and eventually returned it to the wild, and each spring for a number of years it returned to our garden and called a distinctive call we had come to recognise before it left us.

On the bird table a jackdaw will take bread, grain and a variety of seeds once it has become accustomed to visiting you. But in general such visits usually occur when there is a number of jackdaws nesting; they are basically hole-nesters in cliffs, old buildings, chimneys, natural holes in trees and church towers.

A most striking feature of its appearance is its white or pearly-grey eyes which are quite beautiful; the smallest member of the crows it may be, but its grey mantle and black forehead tinged with blue and purple sheen make it quite the most handsome of the family.

It is a noisy bird too, whether its call rings out from a country steeple, blends with the sea wind above the cliffs, or rings out from your roof before it descends to feed.

Lorenz's descriptions of its behaviour show just how little most of us know about the life-style of even a bird as common as the jackdaw, and this should surely encourage every bird lover to spend a little extra time observing our garden birds. There are few more relaxing and profitable ways of spending an hour.

JAY (*Garrulus glandarius*)

Increasingly common in many gardens, it is a noisy, busy, assertive bird that will alight on the bird table, yet remain extremely wary as it feeds. In the wild green world it is a bird of the oak woods, where every autumn it has a riotous time with the acorns. Somehow the word is spread that the crop is plentiful and ripe and jays fly in in large numbers. Perching on the branches they seize an acorn and pouch it, taking as many as four or five, until their throat and crop are bloated from the acorns held in the oesophagus. A quick flight down to the ground, and the acorns are buried, for these birds are great storers and acorns form an important part of their winter diet. Their memory is sufficiently good to guide them back three or four months later. In the meantime, a few of the seeds will have begun to germinate and so it is that jays are one of the main agents in the natural regeneration of our oak woods. It is fascinating to realise that, whilst naturally acorns would roll *down* hill or even remain close to the parent tree, the random burying by jays helps the oak to colonise *up* hill as the birds are no respecters of slope. It is an explicit reminder of the close association that exists between animals and plants within their particular environments and an illustration of the subtle network that embraces us all.

From the bird table point of view, the best we can offer is fruit such as pears,

On the jay's credit side is the fact that it is an important agent in the natural regeneration of oak woods. It buries acorns as a future food resource and many germinate. On the debit side is its liking for birds' eggs and young birds. Whether or not you enjoy its presence in your garden is a personal choice, but none can deny its beauty, its boldness, its noisy arrival and lively movements.

cherries and plums, and nuts such as hazelnuts and beech mast, and occasionally it will take whatever is on the menu, for its natural diet includes small mammals, slugs, worms, insects and, alas, young birds and eggs. Many of the visits to your table to pick up nuts result in the bird burying them to find and eat later on, so not every visit is an actual feeding time. If you watch closely you may well see the bird pouching nuts.

Once a jay recognises your food source it will return again and again, and providing your garden is quiet the bird will approach very close to the house. This 'boldness' is a fairly recently acquired characteristic, for in the past it was ruthlessly shot and trapped on the numerous shooting estates that abounded in the country-side; its sad, dishevelled body hung from many a gamekeeper's gibbet. With the demise of so many shoots, its fear of man is diminishing and, anyway, one wonders to what extent its persecution was justified in terms of pheasant's eggs or chicks.

Magpie (*Pica pica*). Pie

Anyone who has witnessed a 'magpie gathering' in early spring will have little doubt concerning their numbers, even in suburban and urban environments. At such times, they gather together, perhaps in a tall tree, and I have seen as many as seventeen in a fir tree. They alight, one or two hop from branch to branch, some chatter away and a few remain motionless. This may last for a couple of minutes before the whole assembly fly off to a new situation a short distance away, to return again and repeat the performance before dispersing in ones or twos around the neighbourhood. Perhaps such assemblies are part of a pairing behaviour, where paired adults are joined by young unpaired males and females seeking partners.

Magpies frequently visit quiet bird tables, but when our dog is out in the garden the bird's arrival is heralded by a rapid-fire outburst of obviously 'aggressive' chatter. It is interesting, too, that it is the only species that arouses our dog to positive offensive action as she jumps at the tree in which the noisy bird is perched.

In the wild they are nest robbers and take many eggs, but their diet is quite varied and includes caterpillars, insects of many kinds, and woodlice, all gathered from the grass or soil. Nuts, grain and carrion of all kinds are also enjoyed.

So at the bird table the normal offerings will be accepted, especially if there are a few nuts, some grain and bird pie. But the bird will not stay long and it is usually a few quick beakfuls and away.

Nuthatch (*Sitta europaea*)

If your garden is reasonably close to a wood or well-wooded parkland, you may receive visits from this bird. If it comes, it may be in a hurry, picking up a peanut or large seed like a sunflower and making off to the nearest tree. There it wedges the nut into a suitable crevice and, using it as an anvil, breaks the coat open. Sometimes it may make several trips in quick succession, and that probably means it is storing food for future use. But for most of us it may have to remain a bird we see when we go for a woodland walk.

Perhaps we should all be less hasty in judging the magpie as a determined predator. It is, after all, living life in its own natural way and we should enjoy its visits and admire its beauty of form.

SPOTTED FLYCATCHER (*Muscicapa striata*) Cherry-chopper, Cherry sucker, Beam Bird, Beecatcher

A summer visitor to many gardens, having made the long journey from tropical and South Africa. As its name suggests, it is an insect eater and its favourite perch is on a branch from which it is able to fly out, catch a flying insect and return to the branch to eat it. It is a bird worth watching as it makes sudden twists and turns in pursuit of its prey, showing remarkable dexterity on the wing.

Whilst a number of species do make occasional sallies after flying insects, the spotted flycatcher does it repeatedly. Unfortunately, its dependence on insect food may affect its breeding success in cold, wet years when the insect population is low—or grounded. Since it has to cross the Sahara twice every year, the present disastrous state of the Sahel may well, in the long term, have its effect on the numbers visiting us.

Should one settle to nest in your garden, you will have many days of enjoyment watching the bird feeding, especially if you have a pond producing an evening 'gnat-rise'.

TREECREEPER (*Certhia familiaris*)

Essentially this is a bird of mature woodland, for its life is spent—as its name suggests—climbing the trunks of trees searching for the insects that live in the bark fissures and in the moss and lichens.

Just occasionally, when a successful breeding season has sent the numbers up, a few come and explore nearby gardens, especially those with fair-sized trees. A garden without any sizeable tree stands little chance of a visit, for treecreepers need enough bark to press their tail against and thus assist them in climbing. Once into the crown of the tree the birds will 'climb' along branches and even seek insects like caterpillars by clinging to thin sprays of leaves. However, beetles and weevils lurking in camouflaged stillness, spiders in shrouded webs or a moth pupa attached in the spur of a twig provide most of their diet.

Any time you see what appears to be a mouse indulging in tree-climbing, look a little closer; it may well be a treecreeper.

WOOD PIGEON (*Columba palumbus*)

Welcomed by some and resented by others, this is a bird with habits that arouse much controversy. If you happen to grow brassicas, peas or beans, then you may find them ripping away at the fresh green shoots. The problem probably began the previous winter when the pigeons came to your bird table for the grain. Easy pickings become a habit, and if in springtime they see succulent shoots there for the taking, who can blame them for making a detour for a snack?

Incidentally, they *do* secrete 'pigeon's milk', a substance made in the crop, which is fed to their young or 'squabs'; the young birds have specially modified wide beaks to cope with the liquid when it is fed to them. If you are an avid bird gardener you will welcome pigeons along with starlings and herring gulls; after all, it is solely *our* habits which bring them into supposed conflict with *our* interests.

7
THE ART
OF OBSERVATION

With the arrival of spring, every day offers wonderful moments to be enjoyed by anyone who cares for birds, for these are the days when we can observe all the intimate behaviour patterns of the birds around us. Threatening but not destructive territory claiming; tender and beautiful courtship; busy, urgent searching for nest material; the joyful singing from tree-tops. All right, perhaps the singing is part of the warning-off from territory claimed, but can anyone doubt there is a measure of joy expressed in the spring song of a song thrush? Anthropomorphism may well be the bane of the scientific approach, but those of us who have heard the music of a skylark understand that in the small body of a bird dwell emotions akin to what we recognise as joy.

So let us take pleasure in watching the excitement all around the bird garden, and first think about how we can get maximum enjoyment from our watching. Without doubt there is a world of difference between looking at—or simply seeing—a bird and observing one. Watching, to some purpose, is referred to as observation and the art of observation is simply the addition of thinking to seeing. But the thinking must be directed towards the precise happening we are seeing, and we must avoid letting our mind wander. For example, you may see a sparrow behaving in a certain way, but be thinking about what you have to do after lunch. The result is simply that you will not register what you are seeing and almost certainly will not recall it in the future. But if you observe, you will concentrate on what is happening and begin thinking about all the ensuing small actions that add a new dimension to bird-watching.

Perhaps some of your observations will be new to ornithology, for relatively little is known about many aspects of garden bird life. With a little spare time and a notebook you will begin to enjoy your bird garden to the full, and if you join one of the bird societies such as the RSPB or BTO, your interest and knowledge will be even further stimulated.

In observing the birds in your garden you will be joining a great company of enthusiasts many of whom are, or were, great naturalists. Men like Richard Jefferies whose writings inspired so many; W.H. Hudson; Konrad Lorenz who expressed such scientific delight in *King Solomon's Ring*; Niko Tinbergen who introduced many students to fieldwork and who unravelled the behaviour of the herring gull and many other fascinating creatures.

And still today, and indeed always, there will be new and unique observations to be made on even the most common of our garden birds. Foster your sense of wonder and more will be revealed than you ever dreamed possible.

So why not start with a nest box, but remember that first and foremost the

*In the spring keep a look-out for greenfinches performing their courtship feeding ritual as the male offers food to the female. This sort of behaviour can be observed in many garden species and their courtship is fascinating to watch. After Robert Gillmor (*Finches, Ian Newton, Collins New Naturalist Series, 1985*).*

rights of the bird must be considered. Keep your distance whilst it is building and, if you want to watch, select a place some distance from the box and carry out your observation *always* from that one position. Birds quickly become used to your regular presence. Whilst you can take an occasional look into the nest box, try and select a moment when both birds are away, but make it quietly, unobtrusively and quickly depart.

It is best to avoid looking into the box whilst nest-building is in progress and when the young are fairly well developed. In fact, keep your box-opening to an absolute minimum and enjoy your observations from the position you have chosen at a discreet distance.

WATCHING NEST-BUILDING AND FEEDING

When you have time to spare, sit and watch as the birds start building. Do they both carry materials? If not, what is the non-carrier doing meanwhile? What sort of materials are they using and where are they collecting them from? If you feel so inclined, try timing their visits. How many trips per half-hour at different times of the day?

Make a note of what you observe. For example, yesterday a blue tit was busy gathering nest material. It landed on a large fuchsia bush and proceeded to seize pieces of flaking bark and tear them off, gathering five or six lengths before departing for the nest site. It may not seem significant, but the observer can never be certain and so often a number of observations suddenly join together in meaningful information on the life-style of the birds around you. At present the fuchsia bark collecting has been noted along with a host of similar happenings.

Another interesting piece of observation that is easy to set up is to offer nest material. Once you know that sparrows, for instance, are nest-building, offer them a little help. Take some lengths of wool and cut them up into pieces about 7 to 8 cm long. Bundle five or six pieces together and fix them onto a convenient shrub by wedging them in. Fix a number of such bundles and then keep your eye on them. I have seen sparrows and blue tits come and collect them within ten minutes of placing them. In most years early to mid-April seems a good time and, in addition to wool, try a few feathers (if you have any) or some dog's hair (if you have one). As they fly off with your offering you can usually discover their nest site, so that is another bonus.

When the young are being fed it is a time of great activity and you may well be surprised to discover—as you watch—how many visits are made by the pair in an hour. How long does the bird spend inside giving out the food? How often does one of them fly out with a white droppings pellet in its beak? At which part of the day are they busiest? A blue tit alights nearby and then flits into the entrance so quickly it is almost a mere flash, so you have to keep alert even to see its arrival and departure.

To try and discover answers to some of these questions, I spent a few evenings observing a nest box. Sitting against the garden shed a few metres from the box, using a stopwatch, I began to appreciate the work blue tits put into feeding their nestlings. It was not a scientific project, simply a way of learning a little more about my garden birds.

Take, for instance, the question: 'How often do a pair of blue tits individually arrive at the nest with food?' Answer: Average time between visits was 37 seconds (range 26 secs to 59 secs).

My second observation was to try and discover how long each bird spent at the nest box. Answer: nine seconds (range 7 to 12). On many of these visits and departures I saw parents carrying away faeces sacs. In one period of an hour the tits departed the nest box 40 times and on 11 of these occasions were carrying faecal sacs.

From these and many other similar observation periods I began to appreciate how quickly, and presumably efficiently in terms of energy expended, blue tits collect food, in this instance mainly caterpillars but also spiders. They never seemed to rest, were always flying to and fro and only occasionally stayed away from the nest for periods of up to five or six minutes. Perhaps this was when they were feeding themselves—but that is another problem to sort out sometime.

However, referring to *British Tits* by Christopher Perrins, I see he mentions that great tits tend to eat the smaller caterpillars themselves whilst bringing the larger ones to their young; by doing this they make the greatest use of their time and do not waste it by making frequent flights with small items. Maybe blue tits do the same? I wonder.

Based upon such simple and easy observations on a pair of blue tits with nestlings in a garden nest box, one begins to realise how hard a pair of small birds have to work to rear a family. This work rate is further accentuated when one appreciates that each single beakful of insects collected first has to be searched for and found and then caught and carried back to the nest.

WATCHING BATH-TIME AND PREENING

Since so much of the bird's life is involved in flying, the condition of its feathers is most important. Cleanliness and the orderly arrangement of them takes as much as half an hour a day.

Different species have differing ways of bathing; sparrows, for instance, seem to depend on dust baths during the summer and once you have located the shallow, saucer-like depressions in a flowerbed you can watch them next time they dust-bath. When engaged in this activity sparrows are quite sociable and three or more may gather together, each in its own dust-depression.

The purpose of dust-bathing is chiefly to rid the body of parasites such as fleas. They introduce a quantity of dust between their feathers and into their down and then shake and riffle their wings and bodies vigorously, which no doubt scatters the parasites.

Whilst having breakfast this morning I was watching the sixteen sparrows which form our garden colony enjoying a really social occasion. For their 'party' they had chosen a small area of border where the soil was dry and dusty under an overhanging fuchsia bush. First one arrived and pecked around, hopping here and there, and he was then joined by three more, and then others until all sixteen were busily making a party of it. One or two were dust-bathing, leaning forward and rubbing their breast feathers into the dusty soil; whilst doing so each one was busy pecking at the soil, but whether this was to pick up food uncovered by their hectic movements or to swallow pieces of grit for digestion I have no idea. Binoculars would have answered the question, but being cornflake time they were not handy. For some five minutes they dust-bathed, preened and pecked, all the while twittering away in what can only be described as 'social conversation'.

Whether it was as meaningless as similar cackling made at some human social gatherings is left to your imagination. Then suddenly, as if by group decision, they all flew up and alighted on top of some ivy and honeysuckle and started a preening party within two or three inches of one another. As I washed up they dispersed to typical sparrow activities around the garden.

For the more usual form of bathing watch the starlings who, typical of their behaviour, make a real business of it, thoroughly soaking their feathers by dipping breasts into water and scooping it over their bodies using their wings as ladles.

Bathing is well worth watching because the bird is so completely involved in what it is doing.

Preening
This is the equivalent of grooming, and is vital in keeping the feathers in order.

Birds spend periods of the day in sorting out their plumage, and since they are able to use only their beak and feet for this purpose they adopt some quite remarkable positions. Preening is easy to observe and frequently follows a feeding or bathing session.

Birds usually begin preening after bathing or when relaxed and resting, often prior to sleeping. A bird uses its bill to carefully comb its primary feathers so that the tiny barbules fall into place again. It is accomplished by a combination of stroking, as with a comb, and occasional nibbling when a special little problem occurs. If you watch carefully you will be amazed at the care displayed, and the way in which the bird gently quivers its head, pushes and pulls whilst its neck is curved into extraordinary positions. Every so often it will give its head a deft scratch to

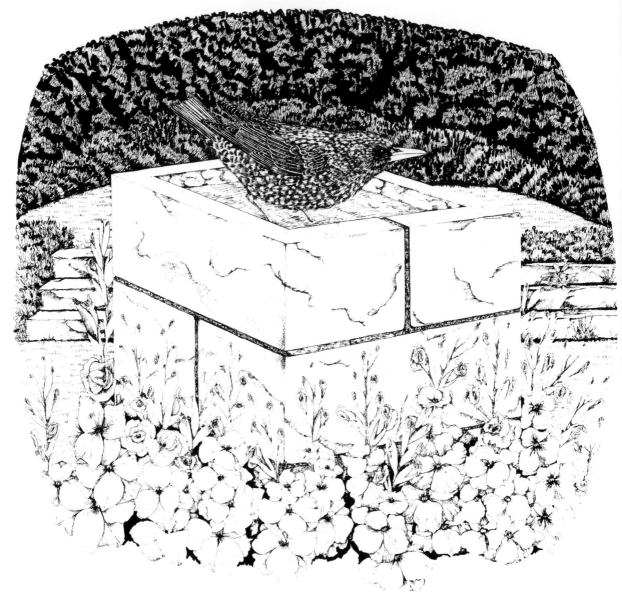

Starlings seem to be particularly fond of bathing but are constantly wary of disturbance. Bath time can be a vulnerable time for an incautious bird.

help things along, or rub its head along its flank to smooth the feathers down. During the preening process a bird will often raise the feather so that it may better explore and clean. Part of preening involves the use of its oil gland which is situated near the tail and the secretion of a preening oil is encouraged by rubbing the gland with its beak. This action transfers the oil onto the beak which is then brushed over the body. Such preening is usually carried out whilst the feathers are damp, perhaps because the moisture assists in the spread of the oil. The resultant thin coating helps to protect the bird in rain and this is why birds can feed in the rain without getting water-logged.

Sunbathing

Many birds enjoy sunbathing, perhaps to encourage the absorption of vitamin D which they later take in when preening. But having watched wrens, sparrows and blackbirds sunbathe I am convinced there is a measure of relaxed comfort involved. They certainly choose a protected, sheltered spot where the sun has warmed either the soil, a wall or a rockery stone. Watch them and perhaps you will agree. Even as I write a company of eight house sparrows are busy preening on the ivy outside my study window and one is sitting quite still facing the sun, obviously enjoying its warmth. One in particular has been meticulous in its cleaning and is engaged in a prolonged nibbling at its back. Perhaps a particularly persistent parasite is lodged there. Who knows? But it is well worth watching.

OBSERVATION AT THE BIRD TABLE

One of the most rewarding aspects of bird-watching for many people is to join up with a recording scheme. In this way your observations help to further the sum total of knowledge concerning their habits and you receive back information that will spur you on to even closer observation. If you are interested in this sort of work, then join the British Trust for Ornithology (see p. 163), and take part in one of their regular surveys.

On the other hand, if you prefer to watch for your own enjoyment, there are still many observations you can make. For instance, you could keep a diary and note down which birds visited your garden and/or bird table whenever you were able to watch. In this way you will soon discover which are the commonest visitors. When do they come? Every month of the year? What time of the day? Do they come in parties, one or two, or singly? Have you observed whether certain species feed together whilst others tend to feed alone? Are you able to recognise one or two individual birds? By making a compartment feeder (p. 63), you can fill each of the pockets with separate seeds—sunflower seeds, millet, peanuts and a wild bird mixture. You can then discover which birds have a preference for a particular food—or conversely do not have a preference. More simply still, if you want to find out which of the offered foods are preferred by the birds visiting your table you can proceed as just described and simply check how quickly a certain food 'disappears'. But remember that as the seasons change different birds will fly in and they may well have different food requirements. And then may come the memorable day when a real stranger appears, perhaps a rare migrant or a local species that has not visited you before. That too can be very exciting, but for me it is the daily routine at the bird table that offers the real interest. Something unusual is always happening and that is the most satisfying reward for any keen observer.

That is only part of the pleasure of a bird garden, but the hours spent in quiet observation, whether in the wild environment or at home, will become more precious as familiarity with your visitors grows. You are entering the birds' world. And it is our world too. Enjoy it.

As you sit quietly observing you will be more conscious of the wildlife around you. Other birds may come and feed nearby, a group of birds begin to scold a nearby cat, you will hear the blackbird's song, maybe a thrush tapping a snail on its anvil, and a whole host of action. It all happens because you found time to 'stand and stare'.

JUST LISTENIN'

So why not listen as you sit and thus enjoy another facet of observation, for certainly there are countless sounds from the bird world all around us. In fact as soon as we relax and tune in to wildlife, it is amazing the sounds we will hear. From the wind in the trees to a pheasant's call; from the high-pitched squeak of a shrew to the distant call of a hunting owl; alarm calls, territorial calls, flight, flock and arrival calls; and amongst the fledglings begging, pleasure and discomfort calls. Suddenly as we sit, still and silent, the green world around us becomes alive, and all because we found time to listen.

Learning bird songs and calls, especially as a guide to identification, is not something one can achieve quickly. It takes patience combined with very close observation. A useful tool in becoming familiar with it is to buy one or more of the very good tapes that are available. Play it over and over again to familiarise yourself, and if you have a walkman then you can even use, for instance, a woodland bird song tape, as a sort of reference book when you visit a summer woodland. Many identification books attempt to describe song in woods with phrases like 'song, a prolonged trill ending in a faint sequence of ti-ti-ti-ti'. This may well help you, but I have always found such written descriptions open to extremely wide interpretation. After all, could you describe the song of an opera singer so that a friend would receive its musical impact simply by reading? The very best way to discover bird song is to go out with a skilled bird-watcher and have some personal tuition. With a little practice you will begin to recognise more and more birds, in much the same way as you recognise people by their different voices. But it is essential to see the singer as well as listening to the song. Start with one particular bird, for example a greenfinch; listen to it many times on your tape; go out into the field and listen; move about, and then quite suddenly you will hear the song and recognise it as the greenfinch flies from its perch in that tree. Singer and song plus observation, and another bird becomes a little more familiar.

The **RSPB**, The Lodge, Sandy, Bedfordshire SG19 2DL (Tel: 0767 680551), supplies some first-class cassettes, including *British Bird Songs and Calls*, Vols. 1 & 2, compiled and edited by Ron Kettle, Curator of Wildlife Sounds at the National Sound Archive. It is a mono cassette (Code 631876), with a speaker naming each song or call.

The RSPB also sells BBC cassettes, and one introduced and produced by Eric

Opposite: *You may not see the night-shift in your garden but many a tawny owl has hunting territory in local gardens. The only sign of its passing may be a soft night call as a pair keep in touch, in what to us is darkness.*

Simms, entitled *Woodland and Garden Birds*, Vols. 1 & 2, is particularly useful as so many of our garden visitors come from woodland. The accompanying notes give location and in many cases actual months when recorded. (Code 631914).

Another BBC cassette in stereo is *Your Favourite Bird Songs*, with commentary listed on tape cover, of a delightful early morning walk in May listening to many well-known songsters. (Code 631930).

Finally, *British Wild Birds* in stereo gives you an opportunity to listen to many of our garden birds singing in their native woodland as well as other habitats. A speaker names each song or call. (Code 631965).

Wild Sounds (formerly Bird Recording Services), PO Box 309, West Byfleet, Surrey KT14 7YA (Tel: 0932 350444), have a stereo recording entitled *Our Favourite Garden Birds*. It is a CD or cassette featuring the familiar birds which live around our homes and gardens. The cassette is announced, the CD unannounced, providing an identification guide to 66 species of Britain and Western Europe, followed by three short stereo concerts to help you practise bird sound recognition.

Another beautifully presented stereo CD or cassette running 52 minutes is *Birds Awakening*. This portrays the spring dawn chorus in the Alpine foothills and includes, among many others, nightingale, great tit, chaffinch, green woodpecker, blackcap and collared dove.

A French publishing company, Sittelle, founded by Jean Claude Roché, one of the most prolific natural sound recordists in the world, has a most interesting catalogue and their UK distributor is Wild Sounds (above). They have some beautiful CDs on topics such as *American Forests and Lakes*, *Forests of the Amazon*, and *African Forests and Savannas*. And as we enter more fully into integration with Europe, how about trying *Tous les Oiseaux d'Europe* (All the Bird Songs of Europe)? It comprises four CDs, each 79 minutes long, with a booklet containing lists and information on 396 breeding birds of Western Europe. They can also be purchased separately.

Wild Sounds is run by Duncan Macdonald. Any time you happen to be in London you could call at the Bird and Wildlife Bookshop, 2–4 Prince's Arcade, Piccadilly, London SW1Y 6DS (Tel: 071–287 1407), which is one of the high street outlets supplied by Wild Sounds and includes many of the Sittelle editions.

And if you happen to be in France, the Sittelle address is Chateaubois, 38350 La Mure, France.

If you want to combine viewing with listening, there is a comprehensive series of five VHS video-tapes available, called *Guide to British Birds*. Covering 230 British birds, the tapes can be ordered from The Red, Green and Blue Company, PO Box 2810, London W6 0PR. Each species is represented by a colour illustration with high quality audio recording of typical calls (from Jean Roché's superb collection *Tous les Oiseaux d'Europe*. Also included are maps indicating European range and on-screen text describing habitat and key identification points in the field. The coverage of the tapes is as follows: Tape 1. Divers to Ducks; Tape 2. Raptors to Phalarope; Tape 3. Skuas to Woodpeckers; Tape 4. Larks to Flycatchers; Tape 5. Tits to Buntings. The tapes are introduced in an accompanying book by Dr Jim Flegg, a past Director of the BTO.

To complete your observations and to extend their value into a fuller understanding of the birds' world, you will probably keep a diary of information and observations, and write these up daily or weekly (a little difficult if you are watching behaviour at the same moment), or spend a while later recalling what happened.

Yet another facet of observation is one's awareness of the seasons, for so much that happens in the bird's world is dependent upon change. For instance, here is an extract from my diary for April 16th:

> . . . sitting amidst a golden spread of celandines and dandelions and a few pale, late primroses, all bright in the early April warm sun. Occasionally a pheasant calls like the creak of a rusty hinge. Among the yellow flowers the bee-fly with tawny, hairy little body hovers on grey-windowed wings with its long tongue reaching into the nectaries of a dandelion. There is a faint continuous drone of pollen-covered honey bees and the louder, deeper drone that heralds the arrival of a bumble bee queen. They are scarce today, but no matter, it's pleasant sitting here and the south east wind carries the scent of fresh grass.
>
> In the bare tree tops a chiff-chaff calls . . .

Each of those small observations helps to evoke the spring and show just a very small part of life's web for that season. A further note from the garden:

> House martins feeding ravenously and queen bumble bees visiting the berberis flowers. Great tit collected dozens of dog's hairs from our lawn. In middle of night a tawny owl was calling from the lime at the end of the garden. I wonder if it's the same one that was mobbed by a blackbird and others earlier in the evening?

OBSERVATION WITH A PURPOSE

One of the most fulfilling ways to enjoy birds is to work with others, by joining an organisation like the British Trust for Ornithology (BTO) and becoming a regular bird recorder. There is something for everyone and you can choose from a wide range of surveys, censuses and enquiries—nearly all of them nationwide.

Interested new members are put in touch with their local regional representative (RR) who will help you to join in. At the same time you can ask to be introduced to regular bird-watchers who will help and encourage you.

The BTO staff will provide field recording cards with notes. Each survey is different: for example, garden bird counts can be daily, nest-recording is from March to July, estuary counts are taken at high tides monthly all the year round.

The BTO's purpose is enjoyable bird-watching with a conservation goal. Members can:

- Learn more about ornithology.
- Make friends.

- Request advice on their own projects and on ornithological problems.
- Receive *BTO News* six times a year.
- Have concessions on *Bird Study* and *Ringing and Migration*, the Trust's two journals.
- Get special offers on books.
- Receive birding gift catalogues.

Contact: BTO, The Nunnery, Nunnery Place, Thetford, Norfolk IP24 2PU.

Another organisation concerned with the protection of birdlife is the Royal Society for the Protection of Birds (RSPB). Amongst its goals:

- It informs people about birds through films, publications, lectures, exhibitions and talks.
- It runs the Young Ornithologists' Club for young people aged 16 and under.
- It investigates environmental effects on birds, advising government and industry.
- It has a national network of local representatives and members' groups in most parts of the United Kingdom.

As a member you will:

- Receive the popular colourful magazine *Birds*, free, four times a year.
- Have free admission to most of the Society's reserves.
- Be eligible to join the countryside network of lively members' groups and attend the annual members' conference and regional meetings with their stimulating, often famous speakers.
- Receive details of the wide range of gifts marketed by the sales department, both mail order and through their shops.
- Find an absorbing interest for yourself and your family.

Contact: RSPB, The Lodge, Sandy, Bedfordshire SG19 2DL.

To obtain further information please send return postage. Like most conservation and research bodies, bird organisations are always in need of funds and your membership and subsequent activity will be of benefit to the societies, yourself, and of course the birds.

GARDEN BIRDS AND EUROPE

Compared to the British Isles, the rest of Europe is enormous and to a highly mobile creature like a bird the range of suitable habitat is equally extensive. Great tits may be found in gardens in Trondheim on the west coast of Norway or in villa gardens in the toe of Italy, and from Ireland through Russia—even to temple gardens in Japan.

Despite all that man has done in the past in clearing the European forests, there remain large areas of unaltered natural vegetation that still encourage birds to breed and thus to visit our gardens. Birds like blackbird, song thrush, chaffinch, greenfinch and robin always showed a preference for woodland edge habitat, so for them the growing number of wild bird gardens provides compensation. As woodlands are cleared, finches and buntings may thrive on the increase in weed seeds. At the same time human dwellings have offered nest sites in exchange for tree-holes for starlings and jackdaws. True adaptors like the robin, blackbird and dunnock have benefited enormously. Thus change is always happening and an affluent, increasingly garden-conscious European population can only be of help to garden birds.

For travelling British bird lovers there is something extremely satisfying in seeing a robin in a French mountain forest; for continentals there is the pleasure of watching an inflow of migrants from Russia's northern forests.

So Europe's garden birds have found widespread habitats to suit their needs—indeed, the tit family is to be found in gardens, especially those in the vicinity of wooded areas, anywhere from the sub-arctic to warm, temperate situations. In contrast, the song thrush favours the western countries of Europe. You *may* be lucky to see one feeding in a Danish garden, but its song will certainly be heard down through western Europe and northern Spain. Whilst habitat, such as forest with thick undergrowth, is a limiting factor, I am tempted to consider the influence of its food on its distribution. It does seem to follow quite closely the range of the helix and cepeae snails. But just as it favours English gardens with plenty of shrubby growth, so on the continent it seeks the same sort of habitat (which includes true forest).

The chaffinch has been much more adventurous and is a resident from the Baltic southwards to Greece and Cyprus, whilst a bird table in Austria may be favoured as often as one in Portugal.

Fruit growing areas throughout Europe provide thick pickings for the bullfinch, although few will be seen south of Rome. However, it is not averse to mountainous areas up to 3,000 metres.

Normally somewhat retiring by nature, the dunnock turns up well inside the Arctic Circle, but may also be known to visit quiet mountain gardens at over 2,000 metres in northern Spain.

I well remember watching a charm of goldfinches feeding on the downy heads of musk thistles in a sunny garden on the hills above Florence. The owners cared little for the birds, yet perhaps if they had put up a bird table and offered some sunflower seeds, greenfinches would have been there too.

Throughout Europe the common starling flocks and roosts after feeding on whatever scraps are put out for it. Incidentally, I am forever intrigued by the possibility that migrant birds like the starling must surely—just occasionally—mimic some exclusively European species. After all, it has been proved that some birds have regional accents, so surely others will have a touch of the estaminet or fjord-talk. Perhaps we should all listen more carefully to those chattering starlings on our TV aerials.

That greatest survivor of all, the house sparrow, will be found almost everywhere man has his habitation, and only in parts of north-central Norway and Sweden does it apparently find conditions unsuitable. However, no doubt those areas are already on its travel agenda. Equally unexpectedly, it is not found in Italian gardens—nor indeed anywhere in that country. Instead the Italian sparrow has occupied the peninsular, although most of us would find that the difference in appearance really tested our powers of observation. Next time you travel down the autostrada look out for them on the picnic sites.

Associated with human offerings of liberal hectares of cultivated grain, the wood pigeon is ubiquitous in such areas providing there are woods, particularly broad-leaved, nearby. A continental garden in such a situation will certainly receive a visit, but many bird lovers seem to prefer a blank space instead of a tick against this bird's name on the visitor list. It was an unfortunate bird in the 1960s when continental—as well as British—farmers sprayed chlorinated hydrocarbons and the seed-eating birds suffered in consequence. I know that farming is not gardening, but birds cannot differentiate between food sources, so although the gardener may feed aflatoxin-free peanuts, there are wider implications in the 'green' world beyond the garden.

A bird extremely partial to human habitation is the collared dove, in occupation from the Spanish border and now moving farther and farther north to gardens and similar habitats from Bergen to Stockholm.

That beautiful dome-nest builder, the long-tailed tit, is represented by three forms in Europe. Up in the north of its range a white-headed form predominates; then south of that area and over most of the continent south of the Baltic (including Britain) the stripe-headed form with a dark breast is seen; in southern Europe another stripe-headed form, but with a grey back, is the one that visits gardens.

A number of garden birds have continental forms, but nearly all of them have such small differences in appearance that to anyone other than specialist ornithologists they look somewhat alike. Nuthatches, for instance, are not quite the same but still closely resemble the occasional visitor to southern English gardens, and if they do visit, for example, a French garden, they will still enjoy the peanuts on offer.

Two species of treecreeper may visit continental gardens but much will depend upon their closeness to certain forests. The Eurasian treecreeper will visit from conifer and montane areas, whereas the short-toed treecreeper prefers open pine, broadleaf and mixed forests. Obviously it is not a lover of Europe's suburbia. Another visitor may be the green woodpecker, flying in from open deciduous woods and from areas with plenty of trees, to enjoy ants on the lawns almost anywhere on the entire continent of Europe; yet it neglects most of north Scotland and Ireland. The great spotted woodpecker tends to favour the higher mountain forests up to 2,000 metres or more, especially in the south of its range.

Perhaps one of the most widely distributed birds is the magpie whose harsh rattle may be heard in any garden from the Arctic Circle south to the Mediterranean providing you have a few tall trees and some shrubs. Absent in north-west Scotland, it is found throughout Europe where it comes into larger gardens. Unfortunately, in many urban areas where houses have replaced large gardens, the loss of trees and a suitable habitat have been followed by a decline in numbers, despite its liking for humankind and its works. Whilst magpies have come under human influence, the jay, now, as ever, depends on oak trees. A European garden near an oak wood will be visited by this garrulous bird, and in south-west France, for instance, invasion movements sometimes occur when the acorns are ripe — with an ensuing slight increase in garden visitors when the crop has been consumed.

The sprightly pied wagtail is resident mainly in the southern half of Europe but breeds anywhere from north of the Arctic Circle and then southwards into northern France, Germany and the Netherlands.

Hiding in and out the undergrowth wherever humans have provided shelter, the tiny wren will sing its song throughout Europe. So too will the robin, but unlike those in British gardens the continental robins are much more shy, especially in France, Spain and Italy where they prefer the woodland to gardens.

It is with some temerity that these few pages attempt to venture onto the continent. But fortunately for travellers or residents who wish to explore further in this wider Europe there is an excellent reference book, *An Atlas of the Birds of the Western Palaearctic* by Colin Harrison, which shows the summer, winter and resident distribution of 639 species of birds in Europe. What more can any wild bird gardener wish for, if he longs to know across which frontiers garden birds, and others, are to be found?

SUPPLIERS OF WILD FLOWER SEEDS

John Chambers, 15 Westleigh Road, Barton Seagrave, Kettering, Northants NN15 5AJ.

Chiltern Seeds, Bortree Stile, Ulverston, Cumbria LA12 7PB.

Samuel Dobie & Son Ltd., Broomhill Way, Torquay, Devon TQ2 7QW.

Emorsgate Seeds, Emorsgate, Terrington St Clement, King's Lynn, Norfolk PE34 4NY.

Mr Fothergill's Seeds Ltd., Kentford, Newmarket, Suffolk CB8 7BR.

Landlife Wild Flowers Ltd., The Old Police Station, Lark Lane, Liverpool L17 8UU.

Naturescape, Little Orchard, Main Street, Whatton-in-the-Vale, Notts NG13 9EP.

Suffolk Herbs, Sawyers Farm, Little Cornard, Sudbury, Suffolk CO10 0NY.

Suttons Seeds, Hele Road, Torquay, Devon TQ2 7QJ.

Thompson & Morgan, London Road, Ipswich IP2 0BA.

Wildseeds, Branas Llandderfel, Gwynnedd LL23 7RF.

BIBLIOGRAPHY

The RSPB Book of Garden Birds, L. Bennett. Hamyln, 1978.
The Birdlife of Britain, P. Hayman and P. Burton. Mitchell Beazley, 1976.
The Popular Handbook of British Birds, P.A.D. Hollom. Witherby, 1980.
New Generation Guide to the Birds of Britain and Europe, Christopher Perrins (General Editor: David Attenborough). Collins, 1987.
British Birds, A.J. Richards. David & Charles, 1979.
The Birds of the British Isles, T.A. Coward. Frederick Warne, 7th ed., 1950.
Birds of Britain, L. Bonhote. Macmillan, 1907.
The Garden Bird Book, D. Glue. Macmillan, 1982.
Birds in the Garden, M. Mockler. Blandford, 1982.
Woodland Birds, E. Simms. New Naturalist Series. Collins, 1971.
Bird Behaviour, R. Burton. Granada, 1985.
A Field Guide to Birds' Nests, B. Campbell and J. Ferguson-Lees. Constable, 1972.
Eggs and Nests of British Birds, F. Finn. Hutchinson, 1910.
Birds as Builders, P. Goodfellow. David & Charles, 1977.
Nests, Eggs and Nestlings of British and European Birds, C. Harrison. Collins, 1975.
Nesting Birds, Eggs and Nestlings, S. Hoeher, trs. W. Reade. Blandford, 1977.
Nestboxes, Field Guide No. 3, J.J.M. Flegg and D.E. Glue. British Trust for Ornithology.
Nestboxes, BTO Guide No. 20, C. du Feu. British Trust for Ornithology, 1985.
British Nesting Birds, W.P. Westell. J.M. Dent, 1919.
The Bird Table Book in Colour, T. Soper. David & Charles, 1977.
The Life of the Robin, D. Lack. Fontana, 1970.
Robin Redbreast, D. Lack. Oxford University Press, 1950.
Robins, C. Mead. Whittet Books, 1984.
British Tits, C. Perrins. New Naturalist Series. Collins, 1979.
British Thrushes, E. Simms. New Naturalist Series. Collins, 1978.
Finches, I. Newton. New Naturalist Series. Collins, 1972.
The Crows, F. Coombs. Batsford, 1978.
Man and Birds, R.K. Murton. New Naturalist Series. Collins, 1971.
Population Trends in British Breeding Birds, J.H. Marchant, R. Hudson, S.P. Carter and P. Whittington. British Trust for Ornithology, 1990.
Birds and Berries, B. Snow and D. Snow. T. & A.D. Poyser, 1988.
Hedges, E. Pollard, M.D. Hooper and N.W. Moore. New Naturalist Series. Collins, 1974.

Guide to the Ferns, Mosses and Lichens of Britain and Northern and Central Europe, H.M. Jahns. Collins, 1983.
The World of Spiders, W.S. Bristowe. New Naturalist Series. Collins, 1958.
The Pattern of Animal Communities, C. Elton. Methuen, 1979.
The Living Garden, G. Ordish. Bodley Head, 1985.
The Ages of Gaia, J. Lovelock. Oxford University Press, 1988.
King Solomon's Ring, K. Lorenz. Methuen, 1952.
The Tree and Shrub Expert, Dr D.G. Hessayon. pbi Publications, 1983.
'Wild Fruits in the Diet of British Thrushes', P.H.T. Hartley. In *British Birds*, 47, 97–107.
An Atlas of the Birds of the Western Palaearctic, C. Harrison. Collins, 1982.

ACKNOWLEDGEMENTS

This book would never have been written but for the innumerable naturalists I have encountered in the field and whose books have been both a pleasure to read and a never-ending source of information. Whatever small knowledge one has on a subject has inevitably been gleaned in many ways, particularly from the birds that visit our garden. The monthly magazine *British Birds*, the British Trust for Ornithology and the RSPB have each been helpful in a variety of ways. My thanks to Robert Gillmor and HarperCollins for permission to use his picture of greenfinch courtship as a reference and to Mark Poole who identified some of the mosses. I also acknowledge the following for permission to use extracts from their books: *The Living Garden* © George Ordish 1985 (The Bodley Head). *Birds of Britain* by Lewis Bonhote 1907 (Macmillan London Ltd). *Population Trends in British Breeding Birds* by J. H. Marchant, R. Hudson, S. P. Carter and P. Whittington (BTO and Nature Conservancy Council). *British Tits* by Dr Christopher Perrins, *Woodland Birds* by Eric Simms, *The World of Spiders* by W. S. Bristowe (all three published by HarperCollins in the New Naturalist Series). *The Pattern of Animal Communities* by Charles Elton (Methuen & Co.). *The Ages of Gaia* by James Lovelock (Oxford University Press). *The Crows* by Franklin Coombs (Batsford Ltd). *A Field Guide to Birds' Nests* by Bruce Campbell and James Ferguson Lees (Constable & Co.). Jayne Netley translated my very rough notes into super colour and line, whilst my daughters Diane and Lynne spent many hours deciphering my writing into typescript.

INDEX

Page numbers in *italic* refer to the illustrations and captions